PUBLIC OPINION
AND FOREIGN POLICY

STUDIES IN
POLITICAL
SCIENCE

PUBLIC OPINION
AND FOREIGN POLICY

An Operational Formulation

JAMES N. ROSENAU
Douglass College, Rutgers University

RANDOM HOUSE
New York

TO MY PARENTS

9

Preface

The analysis here presented is a by-product of an empirical investigation supported by the Center of International Studies of Princeton University. The latter study, to be published under the tentative title of *Opinion-Making and Opinion-Makers in Foreign Policy*, focuses on a 1958 conference sponsored by the White House in an effort to provide the public with information about the foreign aid program and thereby to assist its passage through Congress. The conference was attended by some twelve hundred national leaders from all walks of American life who, it was hoped, would subsequently arouse the public to the need for a flexible and extensive foreign aid program.

In reflecting about the possible consequences of such an occasion, and faced with the task of interpreting great amounts of questionnaire data supplied by the conferees, I had to speculate about how foreign-policy ideas circulate in the United States and the contribution that national leaders make to this process. This study is the result of that speculation. It is what might be called pre-theory since, as indicated in Chapter 7, considerably more thought and investigation are needed before a theory of the relationship between public opinion and foreign policy can be developed.

My indebtedness to the Center of International Studies for its support of this project is extensive and I am happy to be able to acknowledge it in print. The encouragement of the Center's Associate Director, Klaus Knorr, and the constructive criticism of Professor Bernard C. Cohen, who has since moved to the University of Wisconsin, were especially valuable in the formulation and implementation of the project.

In the process of revising this essay as a separate publication several valuable suggestions were made by Professor Harold K. Jacobson of the University of Michigan. Three colleagues at Douglass College, Harry C. Bredemeier, Neil A. McDonald, and Constance E. Smith, also read the manuscript and made helpful comments for which I am grateful.

In addition, it is a pleasure to record my appreciation of the support the Ford Foundation provided through an International Relations Training Fellowship in 1958. As a direct consequence of the Fellowship I had an opportunity to audit Herbert H. Hyman's course in public opinion at Columbia University. More than a few of the ideas developed here had their origin in Professor Hyman's stimulating lectures.

As is evident throughout the work, Gabriel A. Almond is another person to whom many of the ensuing ideas can be traced. Professor Almond's writings on the subject will long serve as pioneer works in the field and I was especially fortunate to have his comments on an earlier draft of the manuscript.

I am also grateful to Miss Carol G. Heines and Mrs. Roberta Weber for their able secretarial assistance.

Virtually each page also reflects the editorial comments, substantive criticisms, and moral support of my wife, Norah.

Of course, none of the foregoing persons or organizations is in any way responsible for the shortcomings of the essay. Any conceptual weaknesses or terminological distortions are my responsibility alone.

James N. Rosenau

New Brunswick, N. J.

Contents

PUBLIC OPINION
AND FOREIGN POLICY

Chapter 1

THE STATE OF THE
FIELD: A CRITIQUE

Few aspects of public affairs lend themselves more readily to impressionistic and faulty analysis than does the relationship between the foreign policies of a nation and the opinions of its citizenry.* This relationship can take so

* Although my primary focus is on the relationship between public opinion and foreign policy, I do not mean to imply a significantly different relationship between public opinion and domestic policy. Postwar technological developments have obliterated long-standing distinctions between domestic and foreign concerns, so that the ensuing discussion might well have been expanded to include both types of policies. No such expansion has been attempted, however, because it would raise many questions and problems that have no direct bearing on foreign policy.

many forms that most of us are quick to see in it the explanation for any policies or situations that run counter to our values or that we do not otherwise comprehend. How much easier it is, for example, to blame the shortcomings of an inadequate policy on "the ignorance of the people" than to analyze critically the process through which this policy was formulated. Or, if our values are better served thereby, the inadequacy can be readily ascribed to the failure of officials to heed or tap "the infinite wisdom of the people." Many Americans view themselves as especially knowledgeable about what their fellow citizens feel, think, and want. Undaunted by precise definitions, empirical evidence, and the complexity of the subject, they are ever ready to explain the course of events by asserting their privileged insights into the "public's mind."

Nor do specialists always exercise sufficient care in analyzing the opinion-policy relationship. All too often they interpret the strengths and weaknesses of a policy in terms of untested assumptions about the impact of an indifferent or an aroused public upon the behavior of officials. No less frequently do they evaluate the end products of the policy-making process in terms of unsubstantiated notions about the way in which presidential leadership contributes to the level of public comprehension and commitment.

The fact is that we have little reliable knowledge about the role of public opinion in shaping foreign policy. American political science has yet to shed extensive light on the key processes through which the opinion-policy relationship operates. We have only a scanty understanding of how external opinions enter and shape the deliberations of officials.[1] Even more superficial is our grasp of how foreign-policy opinions are formed and circulated throughout American society. We know practically nothing about why it is that some situations abroad never become the

subject of public discussion, whereas others take hold
and soon acquire the status of national issues.[2]

To be sure, Gabriel A. Almond touches upon such
matters in his pioneering study of the relationship between
public opinion and foreign policy published in 1950.[3]
However, although great strides have been made in the
communications field since then, for some reason no
attempt has been made to construct a systematic formulation of the opinion-policy relationship which draws both
upon the more durable features of the Almond scheme and
on the more recent developments in communications
research. Almond's formulation, for example, has yet to
be elaborated in terms of recent findings which support the
"two-step flow" hypothesis, according to which opinions in
the United States are first circulated by the mass media and
then passed on by "opinion leaders" through word of
mouth.[4] Indeed, the only innovation introduced since 1950
was provided by Almond himself when, some six years
later, he added the concept of an "attention group." [5]

Even a cursory review of the terminology used to describe the circulation of foreign-policy ideas amply demonstrates the extent to which research in this area remains
undeveloped and ambiguous. Consider, for example, the
term "mass media," which has come to mean newspapers,
magazines, books, television, radio, motion pictures, and
any medium involving communication other than by personal contact. This definition, however, is much too broad
to be useful, since it may extend to professional journals,
technical books, closed-circuit telecasts, and homemade
movies, many of which are too specialized to be called
mass media. Aware of the need for a more limited definition, some analysts have defined "mass media" as the communication of ideas or information (messages) to large
numbers of people simultaneously or in a relatively short
period of time. By emphasizing "mass," which is ordinarily
associated with newspaper, magazine, television, radio, and

motion picture audiences, this definition excludes home-made movies and most closed-circuit telecasts. Yet it still in-cludes highly specialized professional and technical writings that are distributed in densely populated occupations, such as medicine or engineering. Too, by this definition, a lec-ture on the Middle Ages delivered to five hundred college freshmen might be construed as mass communication.

To eliminate the professional journal and the history lec-ture from this category, and thereby reduce mass media to a more meaningful and manageable concept, a few ob-servers have specified that mass-media audiences must be heterogeneous and anonymous as well as large.[6] But even this definition, useful though it may be, does not fully resolve all the difficulties. It fails to provide a basis for classifying media designed for homogeneous and inter-mediate size audiences—like those which read professional journals and attend lectures.[7] While mass media and face-to-face communications are, by most criteria, primary means of transmitting messages, to ignore these other types of communication serves to perpetuate the ambiguity that presently characterizes communications research.

Nor is such ambiguity confined to descriptions of the communications media. Similar confusion prevails with respect to the identification of those persons in the society who are central to the opinion-making process. They have been variously designated as the "elite," [8] the "effective public," [9] the "influentials," [10] the "Great Disseminators," [11] the "issue-makers," [12] the "opinion leaders," [13] the "pres-tigeful leadership,"[14] and the "cosmopolitans." [15] For most analysts all these terms are descriptive of the same charac-teristic: a capacity of individuals to influence the course of events and/or the flow of opinion. Hence many analysts make no distinction between these designations, but use them indiscriminately, changing from one term to another solely on the basis of the stylistic need for variety. Other analysts, aware of a difference between, say, the President of the National Council of Churches of Christ and the smalltown clergyman, attempt to distinguish between those who exercise influence in national affairs (the elite) and those who are influential at the local or community level (opinion leaders). Still others view an opinion leader as a person whose opinions on issues are widely disseminated, whereas another conception posits him as one whose views carry weight in small, intimate groups. Thus, both Walter Lippmann and the woman reader who passes on the contents of his columns to members of her bridge club can be and, in effect, have been classified as opinion leaders.

The conspicuous lack of operational definitions which permit systematic identification of varying types of influential persons can be easily illustrated. It would be difficult, for example, to determine which individuals are among the elite on the basis of the definition that this group constitutes "the articulate, policy-bearing stratum of the population which gives structure to the public." [16] Similar difficulties would doubtless attend an effort to identify members of the effective public when the latter is defined as comprising "persons who, because of their social position, their control over the flow of information, their organizational backing, and their access to officials, exert a strong influence over public moods and attitudes and also over foreign-policy making." [17] Nor is research facilitated by citing "the existence, at all social levels, of unofficial but powerful 'opinion leaders' whose attitudes, however derived, are influential in shaping the opinions of large numbers of their associates." [18] In sum, although these characterizations serve to identify the elite and the effective public as general classes of persons, in no way do they indicate how specific individuals should be categorized.

Much more could be said about the confusion of concepts and lack of precise terminology characteristic of analyses of the opinion-policy relationship. Even so well-established a concept as the "two-step flow" suffers from oversimplification and needs to be re-examined. At the very least it ought to be expanded to account for a "four-step flow" in which the news and interpretation of an event are first carried by, say, a newspaper; this is then read and adapted by opinion-makers, who assert (step 2) their opinions in speeches on the subject that are reported (step 3) by the press and thereupon picked up by "opinion leaders" in the general public who in turn pass (step 4) on the opinions through word-of-mouth.

Our primary purpose, however, is not to review critically the literature of the field. Rather it is to demonstrate the urgent need for a systematic and thorough conceptualization of the opinion-policy relationship, and especially of the processes by which foreign-policy opinions circulate in the United States.[19] Verbal ambiguity is a sign of conceptual difficulties. It suggests that insufficient time and attention have been devoted to perfecting the framework through which phenomena may be examined and interpreted. If a variety of dissimilar means of transmitting messages have come to be considered as mass media, and if reliable identification of the elite cannot be achieved empirically, then presumably a careful and detailed reformulation of the opinion-policy relationship is in order.

Perhaps the reader should be warned at the outset of the considerable detail and seemingly awkward terminology that have often been used to develop and delineate the concepts and categories presented below. This procedure was followed on the grounds that precision is preferable to succinctness and that awkward but exact terminology is preferable to ambiguous prose, no matter how stylistically pleasing. If, for instance, the reader feels that it is belaboring the obvious and overusing jargon to label as "opinion-submitters" those whom he regards as lobbyists, let him pause to consider whether the important distinctions which the new term facilitates are not worth the cumbersome terminology with which he must contend.

Chapter 2

THE FLOW OF INFLUENCE
VERSUS THE FLOW
OF OPINION

Most analyses of the opinion-policy relationship are organized around efforts to trace the flow of influence. Almost every aspect of the relationship can be translated into a question of the direction in which influence is being exercised. In the case of the mass media, for example, investigators are usually concerned with the effects these media have upon their audiences—that is, with the extent to which people are influenced by what they read, hear, and see. Similarly, researchers who explore the interaction patterns of small groups are mainly concerned with the impact of individuals upon each other—that is, with the extent to which one person influences the opinions or behavior of others in face-to-face situations. The question of influence is also a primary concern of those who investi-

gate the role played by opinion leaders in the last stage of
the "two-step flow." As the authors of a well-known study
have put it, "Our central problem was to locate key points
in the transmission of personal influence." [1] Likewise, the
study of elite groups focuses primarily, if not exclusively,
on the investigation of who possesses influence and how
it is wielded.

The primacy of the influence concept is easily explained.
The most baffling and pressing questions in this field are,
after all, those which involve cause and effect. Regardless
of the researcher's purpose, whether it be to improve the
operation of democratic theory or the predictiveness of
scientific theory, ultimately his attention will turn to
questions of causality. He will want to know *why* opinions
circulate as they do, or *why* public policy is responsive to
public opinion in the way that it is. And in considering these
"whys," the researcher unavoidably confronts the problem
of charting the flow of influence, since this is the concept
used to describe causality in social interaction. [2] Thus it
is hardly surprising that virtually every aspect of the
opinion-policy relationship has been cast in an influence
framework.

Yet, despite its importance, the concept of influence lies
at the root of the conceptual and terminological confusion
that prevails in the field. For influence cannot easily be
rendered operational, that is, identified and measured in
terms of concrete behavior undertaken by specific individuals or groups. Let us briefly consider what is involved
in the developing of an operational definition of influence.
If it means anything, influence denotes the *process* by which
the behavior of one individual or group *modifies* the behavior of another individual or group. For influence to be
operative, some form of interaction must occur between
the influencer and the influencee. Thus, in order to identify
influence and assess its potency, the researcher must
examine both the behavior which precipitated the influence
and the behavior to which that influence may have con-

tributed, and then he must estimate what the latter behavior might have been if it had not been modified by the influence. The measurement of "might-have-beens," however, is possible only through the manipulation of variables in controlled experiments, and while there is an ever-growing body of reliable experimental data on the operation of influence in face-to-face situations,[3] this method cannot be used to assess the opinion-policy relationship. One cannot manipulate the variables that would reveal which groups or persons in American society exercise influence over the formulation of foreign policy. Rather, the most one can do is to examine the behavior which appears to be a function of the opinion-policy relationship, and then to deduce from that behavior those factors which seem to have been responsible for the influence in question.

In other words, we cannot *observe* the influences that underlie the formation of public opinion and its effect upon public policy; we can only observe behavior and *infer* therefrom which influences are operative. If, for example, we wish to examine the influence that elite groups exert over public opinion and public policy, we must determine who the members of the elite are and which of their many activities constitute the exercise of influence over the public and/or the policy-makers. To do this, we must also identify the relevant segments of the public and of the policy-making organization, and then specify which of the former's many opinions and the latter's many decisions constitute responses to the activities of the elite. Or, if we are interested in tracing the flow of influence from the elite to the public, and thence to officials, we must determine what behavior of each of the three groups is linked together in the interaction sequence that forms the process of influence.

Confronted with these inherent difficulties in the concept of influence, the researcher has three alternatives: (1) he can attempt to overcome the difficulties by seeking to identify and measure influence; (2) he can ignore them; or

(3) he can avoid them by employing more manageable concepts. The first alternative holds out little promise of success. Our empirical knowledge of the motives and attitudes that mediate the behavior from which we must infer the presence of influence is so scanty that the inferential analysis would inevitably border upon guesswork.* In other words, to confine ourselves to the motivational and attitudinal data which are well established and from which reliable inferences may be drawn would be to so narrow the scope of our inquiry as to shed little light on the opinion-policy relationship.[4]

A second way of coping with the difficulties involved is to ignore them—that is, simply not to specify the concrete behavior from which influence is inferred. This is the method used by most observers, and it is also responsible for much of the conceptual and terminological confusion which has plagued analyses of the opinion-policy relationship. For the failure to posit influence as an interaction between influencer and influencee inescapably fosters the view that influence has an existence of its own, apart from the individuals or groups who employ or experience it. At worst, influence comes to be viewed as an intangible force that plays upon men and determines the course of events; at best, it is regarded as a quality possessed by some persons (the influential) and not by others —an "it" which is exerted, exercised, and/or wielded by

* To be sure, there are techniques available which reduce the area of guesswork, notably those developed by Katz and Lazarsfeld in *Personal Influence* (*op. cit.*, Part Two). Focusing on the interaction sequence that forms the process of influence, these researchers asked their respondents (women in a Midwestern community) to designate the persons who advised them on a particular question, and then checked these accounts against those of the designatees. For obvious reasons, however, the application of this technique to interaction sequences involving government officials would prove extremely difficult, if not impossible.

the possessors, and which is felt, heeded, and/or resisted
by those against whom "it" is directed. Such a conception
conduces to ambiguity because it provides no means of
identifying, observing, or measuring the presence of influence. Where does one look for it: on the person of the
possessors? In the positions they hold? In the skills they
have acquired? After all, if influence is a possessed quality,
then those who possess it must be distinguishable from
those who are not so fortunate. The search for these distinguishing traits usually produces ambiguous definitions.
Having committed himself to look only at the possessors of
influence, the observer must inevitably fall back on traits
such as prestige, status, power, or effectiveness.*

Such characteristics, however, beg the question of how
the influential are to be identified. They merely alter the
problem to one of specifying the criteria of prestige, status,
power, or effectiveness—qualities which themselves are no
more easily observed or defined than is influence. To be
sure, ambiguity could be minimized by defining influence
in terms of very specific and measurable qualities. One
could, for example, define as influential all persons who
control a newspaper, who head organizations composed of
more than five hundred thousand members, or who earn
at least a million dollars annually. But such precise criteria give rise to other difficulties which defy resolution.
Most important, such precision is accompanied by a false
inclusiveness—that is, by the necessity of viewing *all*

* Or he can fall back on the widely used technique of asking
a panel of knowledgeable citizens to name those whom they
regard as the most influential members of the community.
However, while this method has produced stimulating findings
(see Floyd Hunter, *Community Power Structure,* University of
North Carolina Press, Chapel Hill, 1953), it does not eliminate
or by-pass the problems which arise when influence is equated
with possessed qualities, but merely transfers from the researcher to the panel members the responsibility for determining who possesses the qualities which constitute influence.

newspaper publishers, organizational leaders, and million-aires as influential, whereas in fact some may be inactive, unconcerned, or otherwise unwilling to utilize the influence which has been attributed to them. In short, the designation of all persons in a particular category as influential no more facilitates the identification and measurement of influence than does the notion that influentiality accrues to those who are prestigeful or powerful.

Nor can the problem be overcome through a com-promise in which some, but not all, of the key components of influence are made operational—that is, through a definition which posits a process of interaction between influencer and influencee, making identification of the latter contingent on observed changes in behavior, but continuing to identify the former by means of certain pos-sessed attributes. The insufficiency of partially operational concepts is readily illustrated in the following attempt to find a middle ground between the two alternatives out-lined above:

> In short, if a group continues to be regarded as politically significant, and if the policies which it favors continue to prevail, then we may reasonably infer that it is more influ-ential in politics than some other group for which these conditions do not hold, or hold only to a markedly lesser degree. Influence is thus inferred provisionally from repeated association with prevailing policies, together with the con-tinuing enjoyment of substantial status and prestige.[5]

On the surface, this definition of influence seems to render the concept manageable. Not only does it emphasize the interactive nature of influence by focusing on "repeated association," but in the phrase "prevailing policies" it also provides behavioral criteria for identifying and assessing the influencee's role in the interaction sequence. Empirical application of the definition, however, is bound to produce considerable confusion. The role of the influencer is not formulated in behavioral terms, but is rather a consequence of being "regarded as politically significant." And how does one uncover the presence of political significance? According to the definition, it is to be found among those groups that have "substantial status and prestige." Thus one is again led to look for possessed qualities which remain undefined and which therefore negate the apparent utility of the overall conception.

But, it might be asked, cannot these difficulties be resolved by simply formulating a more precise definition of the possessed qualities which are equated with influence? If, for example, the criteria of status or prestige were specified, then could we not systematically apply the influence concept to empirical data without having to trace complex interaction sequences? Logical as this reasoning may seem, it does not provide a way out of the dilemma. For the only two methods of operationalizing such qualities as status and prestige present many of the same difficulties that attend efforts to delineate the flow of influence. One method is to adopt specific and objective indices which are presumed to reflect these qualities; the other is to focus upon the subjective phenomena whereby high status or prestige is accorded to those who possess it. The former procedure requires the use of indices such as occupational role, organizational size, and annual income, measures which have already been shown to include persons who may never utilize the influence that is presumed to derive from these characteristics. The latter technique necessitates identifying and investigating those deferential attitudes and actions on the part of the community through which high status and prestige are accorded to particular persons. This method, in other words, involves an inferential analysis of behavior which is certainly no less complex than that from which the presence of influence is deduced. Indeed, the whole community must be examined, and not just the influencees, if ~~prestigeful~~ persons are to be located as a means of identifying those who are influential.

There is a third alternative open to the researcher who

feels that it is premature to chart the flow of influence in behavioral terms, yet immature to trace it in any other way. Instead of coping with the difficulties of measuring influence in terms of behavior, and rather than submitting to the ambiguities which arise when influence is related to certain attributes, he can abandon the concept of influence altogether, and substitute one which is sufficiently manageable to permit a wide-ranging empirical analysis of the opinion-policy relationship. Such a procedure has been followed here.

The ensuing conceptualization has been organized around a particular behavior: the transmission of opinion. Any set of ideas, either informational or judgmental, about any aspect of the world scene is considered to constitute a foreign-policy opinion.* Whatever form the act of communicating these ideas or opinions may take, it can always be observed, categorized, and measured. Individuals and groups can be identified and compared in terms of their performance, both qualitatively and quantitatively, of this type of action. Thus, by distinguishing and classifying the various participants in the opinion-policy relationship according to the form which their communicative behavior takes, it should be possible to avoid the difficulties of measuring influence and the confusion that accompanies efforts to identify possessed qualities.

Equally important, the act of transmitting opinion is necessary to the existence of the opinion-policy relationship. That is, unless opinions about an issue circulate within the public, and between it and the government, neither party to the relationship can modify the behavior of the other, and consequently the relationship does not material-

---

* Since our purposes do not require us to distinguish between attitudes and opinions, this broad definition of foreign-policy opinion has been intentionally designed to include both types of psychological phenomena, thereby avoiding the confusion which usually results from efforts to operationalize the attitude-opinion distinction.

ize in so far as that particular issue is concerned. By abandoning the influence concept, in other words, we do not remove ourselves so far from the opinion-policy relationship as to preclude analysis of it.

This is not, however, to define the opinion-policy relationship as simply the communications system which links members of the public to each other and to their officials. The character of the relationship, as distinguished from the fact of its existence, is determined by the flow of influence, by the processes of interaction through which the public does or does not modify the behavior of its policy-makers. To trace the flow of opinions between citizens and officeholders is not to describe how one exercises influence over the other. Opinions can and do circulate without corresponding modifications of behavior. The official who rejects an opinion that has been transmitted to him illustrates how opinion and influence may *not* flow together. Indeed, it is even possible for an official to cut off the flow of influence at the same time that he is perpetuating the flow of opinion. He could, for example, reintroduce the rejected opinion into the channels of communication by including it in a speech as illustrative of the kind of thinking to which he is opposed. In short, influence cannot be operative without the prior transmission of opinion, whereas the latter can occur independently of the former.

It follows that in organizing our analysis around the act of transmitting opinion, we are establishing a framework within which the flow of influence is confined. It is hoped that the systematic construction and application of this framework will facilitate efforts to surmount the difficulties that presently attend use of the influence concept. By charting the circulation of foreign-policy opinions in American society, we should be in a better position to comprehend and assess the dynamics whereby public policy and public opinion become functions of each other. Equally important, by identifying and classifying opinion-makers we should pave the way for a more systematic analysis of those persons in our society who guide the development of public opinion and shape the formulation of foreign policy.

In sum, having removed the causal agent from the opinion-policy relationship by sidestepping the influence concept, we have probably deprived ourselves of the where-withal to theorize about the relationship. In so doing, however, we allow for clarification of the concepts and processes that, as indicated in Chapter 7, should form the basis of a general theory of how the public and its policy-makers will affect each other in various types of situations. From the outset, then, what follows has been deliberately developed as a descriptive conceptual framework rather than as a predictive theoretical one.

Chapter 3

THE OPINION-POLICY

RELATIONSHIP

It is useful to view the relationship between public opinion*
and foreign policy as being composed of three distinctly
different, but closely related, social processes—that is,
as three separate systems of interaction between discrete
individuals. One is the *governmental decision-making
process* through which foreign policy is formulated and
into which existing public opinion is integrated by the

* As indicated below, the "public" is not equated with the
citizenry of the nation. Rather, only those who hold opinions
about an issue are considered to constitute the "public" with
respect to that issue. In this sense the public, "as distinct from
the small group, . . . is a transitory, impersonal aggregate
that is organized around a particular issue" (Davison, *op. cit.*,
p. 106). Hence the phrase "public opinion" is used to refer
generally to the different publics that have formed around the
various issues preoccupying the nation at any moment.

officials responsible for the conduct of policy (henceforth designated as the decision-makers or policy-makers). Another is the *opinion-submitting process* that occurs whenever opinions are conveyed to or impressed upon decision-makers by individual members or segments of the public (hereafter called the opinion-submitters). And thirdly, there is the *opinion-making process* whereby ideas about foreign-policy issues are formed and circulated in American society (through the interaction of what shall be referred to as opinion-holders and opinion-makers, the former being the entire citizenry and the latter those citizens who introduce opinions into the impersonal channels of the communications system).

It must be emphasized that the first and the last of these processes are independent systems of interaction, which is to say that both can occur irrespective of any linkage with the other. Opinions about foreign-policy issues can be and are circulated without coming to the attention of decision-makers. Because the opinion-submitting process is not always initiated, government does not necessarily experience every throb in the circulatory system whereby opinions are disseminated throughout the society. Likewise, decision-makers can and do conduct their deliberations and arrive at foreign-policy decisions without knowledge of the existing state of public opinion, either because the latter has not been conveyed to them or because, in the absence of an opinion-submitting process, they do not, consciously or otherwise, perceive its existence.

The opinion-submitting process, then, derives from the other two processes. If the decision-making process is inaccessible, or if the opinion-making process is quiescent or not governmentally oriented, there can be no opinion-submitting process. In this dependent sense, of course, the opinion-submitting process is merely an aspect of the opinion-making process. Yet, by analyzing it separately, constant attention is drawn to the crucial fact that the other two processes can operate independently of each other.

Why is the independence of the decision-making and

opinion-making processes so crucial? Precisely because the opinion-policy relationship is defined in terms of a linkage between these two processes. Their interdependence, as distinguished from independence, is necessary for the relationship to exist at any particular moment. This analytic definition, while lacking an operational basis, has the advantage of freeing us from the value definition that opinion and policy *ought* to be articulated in harmony with each other. It forces us to posit the existence of the relationship as a hypothesis that has to be tested, rather than as an existing situation which calls only for description.

Having conceptually (but not empirically) established that the opinion-policy relationship can cease to exist even as its components continue to function, let us turn to its actual operation, to the varying linkages and sequences through which the relationship is formed and sustained. It must first be noted that the definition above does not posit a relationship in which policy is always a reflection of opinion. The definition merely asserts that the relationship cannot exist unless the two processes are linked together in some fashion. As can be seen in the diagrammatic presentation of the relationship (below), linkage can occur in several other sequences besides the one which reflects classical democratic theory ($8 \rightarrow 9 \rightarrow 10$ on the diagram). Moreover, policy may not reflect opinion even if such a sequence is initiated; the resulting linkage might be an entirely negative one in which decision-makers reject the policy alternatives presented by the other two processes.

Nor does the opinion-submitting process have to intervene for linkage to occur. The definition also makes allowance for the special sequence whereby decision-makers, consciously (linkage 1) or otherwise (2), circumvent the opinion-submitting process by engaging in their own estimates of the prevailing state of opinion. Indeed, it may well be that the intervention of the submission process is more atypical than typical. Conceivably the perceptual antennae of decision-makers are more sensitive to unsolicited evidences of opinion than to representations made

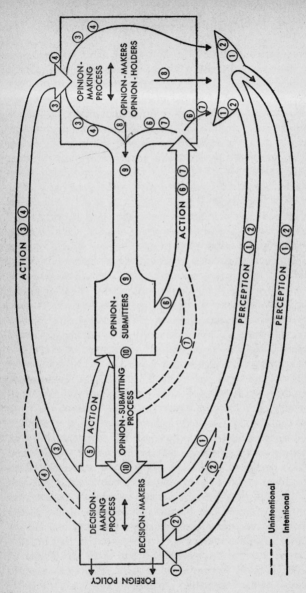

22

by opinion-submitters. Recent history is filled with instances in which decision-makers appear to have taken into account a larger "climate" of opinion that, rightly or wrongly, they somehow perceived to be operative as latent public attitudes or as manifest but unstructured majorities which opinion-submitters failed to articulate. In other words, opinions do not have to be submitted for policy to be linked to them. Contrary to the simple model of democratic value theory $(8 \rightarrow 9 \rightarrow 10)$, the opinion-policy relationship can be initiated by, and even confined to, the perceptions of decision-makers (1 or 2).

There is still another way in which decision-makers can initiate the relationship. Besides perceptual circumvention of the opinion-submitting process, they can also activate a sequence that runs from decision-making to opinion-making to opinion-submitting to decision-making (3, $4 \rightarrow 8 \rightarrow 9 \rightarrow 10$). This major variation from the democratic-value model centers around the fact that the federal government is itself a primary contributor to the opinion-making process. The speeches of Congressmen, the messages of the President, and the press releases of various departments and agencies are but a few of the many ways in which opinions are fed to the public. Decision-makers, in other words, often become opinion-makers. This multiplicity of roles may result from the unintentional contribution which decision-makers make to the opinion-making process (4) by virtue of their participation in the decision-making process; that is, interaction among them which occurs in public, as in legislative hearings or Congressional debates, can serve an unanticipated opinion-making function. Or, as is perhaps more often the case, the shifting of roles can be the consequence of intentional efforts by decision-makers to shape the direction and intensity of public opinion (3). The conviction that the success of a particular policy depends upon the degree of public support it enjoys, or at least upon the extent to which public opposition is minimized, leads decision-makers to assume the role of opinion-makers in order to facilitate the subsequent performance of their tasks as decision-makers. They may simply attempt to foster a "climate" of opinion more favorable to their contemplated policy, hoping in this way to affect the perceptions of other decision-makers who are either opposed to the projected proposal or not yet persuaded of its wisdom $(4 \rightarrow 1,2)$. Or, they may try to convince their colleagues by engaging in opinion-making designed to alter the opinion-submitting process in such a way as to reduce the volume of negative submissions or to increase the flow of positive submissions $(4 \rightarrow 8 \rightarrow 9 \rightarrow 10)$. Rivalry and disagreement between the legislative and executive branches of the government is frequently channeled along these circuitous opinion-making routes, each branch seeking to prove to the other that its position is supported or accepted by the "public."

While decision-makers can promote the submissions process indirectly by acting as opinion-makers, they cannot, by definition, shift into the opinion-submitting role itself. This would, so to speak, involve them in making representations to themselves or to each other, an activity which is virtually the essence of decision-making and thus cannot usefully be construed as opinion-submitting. There is, however, one way in which decision-makers can initiate the submission of opinions directly, namely by soliciting them $(5 \rightarrow 10)$. As illustrated by the Congressman who takes a poll of his constituency, or by the agency head who calls in outsiders for advice, decision-makers can cause opinion-holders to become opinion-submitters even if they cannot shift into this role themselves. At least three reasons would seem to lead decision-makers to solicit opinions in this direct fashion: (1) In the absence of any other linkages, they may want to create (or maintain) the opinion-policy relationship because of a conviction that it ought to exist. (2) Distrustful of their own capacity to perceive accurately the inarticulate "climate" of opinion, yet doubtful of the representativeness of the "self-interested" opinions currently being submitted, they may turn to the solicitation of "disinterested" opinion. (3) They may want to bolster a particular position they may have taken in the decision-making process by citing otherwise unattainable evidence that the "public" shares their viewpoint.

Normally, of course, the submission of opinions is not so much a response to the solicitations of decision-makers as it is a process initiated voluntarily ($9 \rightarrow 10$), either by professional opinion-submitters or by opinion-holders temporarily performing this role. The latter type refers to those members of the public who write letters to decision-makers or in some other way submit their personal opinions. They speak for themselves alone and only on irregular occasions. Once their views have been submitted, they return immediately to opinion-holding, until such time as circumstances (including the urgings of opinion-makers) again move them to shift roles. Professional opinion-submitters, on the other hand, are continuously attempting to establish contact with decision-makers. They submit opinions on behalf of large aggregates or organizations, either because they are specifically employed to do so (as lobbyists) or because their responsibilities include representing the organizational interests in the halls of government (as, say, presidents or chairmen).

The professional submitters are thus a vital link between the public and the decision-makers, introducing meaning and reality into the classic democratic model ($8 \rightarrow 9 \rightarrow 10$). But their activities are not limited to those of mere middlemen. They too can initiate a sequence in the opinion-policy relationship, one that runs from opinion-submitting to opinion-making, and thence back to decision-making via any of the linkages previously described ($6,7 \rightarrow 8 \rightarrow 9 \rightarrow 10$ or $6,7 \rightarrow 1,2$). Such a sequence develops when professional submitters assume the role of opinion-makers. Like decision-makers, and for similar reasons, they frequently make this shift, either unintentionally or purposely. As occupants of organizational positions that command respect among segments of the public, professional submitters may unintentionally foster opinion-making (7) whenever they employ public rather than private means of participating in the opinion-submitting process. Under these circumstances their audience is not necessarily confined to decision-makers, so that their statements may have unanticipated opinion-making consequences. It may even be that the views they express in such open and publicized forums as legislative hearings have a greater impact upon members of the public than upon the decision-makers for whom they were intended.

More frequently, professional submitters intentionally turn to opinion-making (6). Persuaded that decision-makers will heed them more closely if they can provide evidence of support for their positions, professional submitters easily become accustomed to stepping into the role of opinion-makers. Moreover, because of their organizational affiliation, a wide variety of opinion-making techniques are at their disposal. Through publicity releases, they may attempt to alter the "climate" of opinion in such a way that decision-makers who perceive it will be more receptive to their subsequent submissions ($6 \rightarrow 8 \rightarrow 1,2$). Or they may try to extend the opinion-submitting process itself by encouraging a temporary shift in role on the part of opinion-holders ($6 \rightarrow 8 \rightarrow 9 \rightarrow 10$). They may even facilitate such a shift by providing opinion-holders, especially those within their own organizations, with mimeographed letters that have only to be signed and mailed to decision-makers. In short, the professional opinion-submitter often deliberately becomes a well-equipped opinion-maker in order to make himself more effective in the former capacity.

Thus far, attention has been focused on the varying sequences and role shifts through which the decision-maker and the opinion-submitter initiate the opinion-policy relationship. Now we must turn to the opinion-makers and the opinion-holders, without whom the relationship cannot be consummated. We need to clarify the distinction between them, to differentiate various types within each group, and to delineate the several channels through which opinions circulate and come to be held.

Chapter 4

THE STRATIFICATION
OF THE PUBLIC

Americans differ widely in the manner and extent of their participation in the opinion-making process. Differences in the *manner* of participation can be traced along a motivation-information scale ranging from opinion-holders who are totally unconcerned and uninformed about world affairs to those who are greatly concerned and well-informed about such matters. Differences in the *extent* of participation can be analyzed in terms of accessibility to the personal (face-to-face) and impersonal channels that form the communications system through which opinions circulate. The accessibility scale is conceived to range from opinion-holders who are unable to transmit opinions beyond the circle of their acquaintances to those who can disseminate their views widely among persons whom they do not know. These two scales form the basis of the stratification of the public developed below. First the accessibility scale is used to draw a distinction between opinion-holders and opinion-makers. The motivation-information scale is then employed as a means of distinguishing between two basic types of opinion-holders. Subsequently we shall return to the accessibility scale and use it to differentiate between sixteen main types and many secondary types of opinion-makers.

Opinion-holders are those persons in the society who, on a given issue or in general, cannot circulate opinions to persons with whom they are not acquainted. They may disseminate opinions on a face-to-face basis, but they have no access to the impersonal channels of the circulatory system. *Opinion-makers,* on the other hand, are those who, by virtue of their position of leadership in the society, have access to the impersonal channels. Opinion-makers may vary considerably in the extent of their access, and in respect to the number of issues about which they can circulate opinions to unknown persons, but on a particular issue all of them are above the zero point on the accessibility scale. While it follows that some persons may be opinion-holders on some issues and opinion-makers on others, the ensuing discussion is based on the premise that the vast majority of opinion-holders are not able to shift into an opinion-making role at any time. Note will be taken of those who can and do make such a shift when we come to examine the opinion-makers more closely in Chapter 5.

In equating opinion-making with access to the impersonal channels, we do not mean to minimize the importance of face-to-face communication or to deny the substantial evidence that it is a highly effective form of communication. On the contrary, there is every reason to emphasize that the processes of influence have been found to operate more extensively in face-to-face situations than in impersonal ones,[1] and that therefore the opinions which opinion-holders internalize and adopt are usually those which were transmitted to them through some personal means. In other words, we do not deny that every opinion-holder has some access to the circulatory system in the sense that potentially he can perpetuate the flow of opinion by merely expressing himself in the presence of others. Indeed, it is quite appropriate that opinion-holders who sustain the circulation of opinion in this manner be regarded as "opinion leaders," a designation which stresses the central role played by those who relay ideas and information from the impersonal channels to the personal ones.*

Notwithstanding the centrality of their role, however, it seems preferable not to view opinion leaders as opinion-makers nor to designate as opinion-making the communicative activity of those persons whose access is limited to the personal channels of the circulatory system. Two major considerations make it advisable to restrict the definition of opinion-making to the activity of those individuals who have access to impersonal channels. In the first place, it will be recalled that we are concerned here with charting how and where opinions flow through the communications system, not with depicting how and where they come to be held. In this sense it is the impersonal channels that constitute the main arteries of the circulatory system. Through them, opinions are distributed throughout the society regardless of whether they are picked up and internalized by individual opinion-holders. Opinions will not circulate very far, on the other hand, if

---

* The designation "opinion leader" has been explicitly applied to performers of this relay function by Katz and Lazarsfeld, *op. cit.*, pp. 137-38, and it is in this sense that we shall use the designation on the few occasions when we need to take note of face-to-face communication among opinion-holders. If opinion-holders were more central to our focus, it would probably be necessary to develop new terminology (including, say, "opinion-relayer"), so as to delineate more clearly the various types of access to personal channels.

those expressing them fail to modify—that is, influence—the viewpoints of their listeners. Through the personal channels may flow important pulsations of influence, but, from the point of view of opinion circulation, they are, so to speak, the small vessels which carry the blood to the extremities of the organism.

A second and closely related reason why those who transmit opinions exclusively by face-to-face means are not considered opinion-makers stems from the conception that the circulatory system functions via a "two-step flow," in which opinions first move through its impersonal channels and are then passed on through personal channels. If this is the case, and all the evidence justifies such a conception, it then follows that those who initiate the first step of the sequence are also those who give structure, informational content, and judgmental direction to the opinions which enter the communications system. In other words, the opinions which circulate are given form—are "made"—by those who introduce them into the impersonal channels. Hence it is appropriate to designate persons who have access to these channels as opinion-makers, and to regard everyone else as opinion-holders—that is, as potential recipients of the opinions which circulate.*

* At this point, I make no distinction between nonopinion-makers who have highly structured opinions about a particular foreign-policy issue and those who have no opinions whatsoever. Both are considered opinion-holders in order to emphasize that those who lack opinions may be just as relevant to the opinion-policy relationship as those who adhere to a point of view. In this sense, lack of ideas or information about an issue is considered to be a form of opinion. Moreover, by designating all nonopinion-makers as opinion-holders, we also make the point that behavior has to occur for opinions to be acquired, that potentially all citizens may be aroused to dip into the circulatory system for ideas and information. Of course, the distinction between the two types of opinion-holders cannot be entirely overlooked; it is accounted for below by

To be sure, opinion-holders can be said to form or "make" opinions whenever they dip into the circulatory system and internalize as their own one set of opinions rather than another. Opinions which become internalized in this fashion, however, already possess structure, content, and direction, so that opinion-forming in the creative sense does not accompany the process by which most opinion-holders develop their opinions. Similarly, the "making" of opinion does not necessarily occur when, say, two opinion-holders argue about which of several alternatives should be followed with respect to a particular foreign-policy issue. Even if one of them is ultimately convinced by the other in this face-to-face situation, such a debate does not constitute opinion-making because ordinarily the disputed alternatives have been previously formulated and have reached the disputants through prior throbs of the circulatory system. In short, it is henceforth assumed that opinions are formed *before* they circulate widely; that only opinion-makers formulate the opinions which are widely disseminated; and that little modification occurs in the structure, content, and direction of opinions once they circulate beyond the ranks of opinion-makers.*

---

an application of the motivation-information scale in which the opinion-holding public is subdivided into the attentive and mass publics.

* This point suggests that the opinion-making process is composed of two subprocesses: opinion-forming and opinion-circulating. The former refers to the interaction which takes place between opinion-makers (either through personal or impersonal channels) and which results in the development of diverse interpretations and judgments of particular issues. The latter refers to the communicative activity of opinion-makers whereby they introduce opinions into the impersonal channels that extend beyond their ranks. Although we shall have occasion to note that opinion-forming may not be followed by opinion-circulating, it is assumed that normally the two subprocesses overlap and unfold sequentially. Accordingly, so as

This does not mean that opinion-makers are necessarily more influential than the opinion leaders who subsequently reroute their opinions from the impersonal to the personal channels of communication. As previously noted, influence is considered to be a process of interaction in which the behavior of the influencer modifies the behavior of the influence. In this sense, those who are responsible for the way in which opinion-holders internalize opinions may be just as influential as those who are responsible for the introduction of opinions into the circulatory system. Opinion-makers may often, but not always, perform the former as well as the latter function. The exercise of influence is not, to repeat, an automatic derivative of participation in the opinion-making process.

Nor does the distinction between opinion-makers and opinion-holders necessarily mean that the former are more knowledgeable about world affairs than the latter. The fact that many opinion-holders are dependent upon them for ideas and information does not necessarily lead opinion-makers to formulate sound or elaborate opinions. In some cases such a dependence may even require the formulation of opinions which, to the outside observer, seem to have little relevance to the world scene. Thus, depending upon the particular positions they occupy, some opinion-makers appear to be well informed and others uninformed. In their opinions, some may reflect the world they see while others may reflect the world they believe ought to exist. Some will advance their opinions as tentative formulations; others will insist that they have developed a blueprint for immediate action. Some may circulate opinions about every major issue, while others may confine their opinion-making activity to selected issues, either because they choose to do so or because their positions limit

to avoid unnecessary complexity, this breakdown of the opinion-making process has not, except as otherwise noted, been made a part of the ensuing analysis.

their access to the impersonal channels. Some may not purposely utilize their access to the impersonal channels, but may unintentionally have their opinions circulated because others, such as journalists, specialize in circulating the views of all opinion-makers as well as their own. In other words, opinion-makers are not homogeneous in either outlook or behavior.

Having used the accessibility scale to identify the opinion-makers, we are now in a position to complete the stratification of the public by introducing the motivation-information scale and differentiating between two basic types of opinion-holders. This latter distinction leads to a conception of American society that places all of its members in one of three strata. Together, these strata form a pyramidal structure that constitutes the "public" for any foreign-policy issue at any moment in time. While the composition and size of each stratum may vary somewhat as the issues vary through time,[2] all three will be present in a hierarchical arrangement whenever the opinion-policy relationship is activated and a public forms around a particular issue. As previously implied, opinions relative to the issue will circulate both vertically between the strata and horizontally within them. We shall return to these downward and sideward channels of communication after we have examined the characteristics of each stratum.

At the base of the pyramid, and comprising the greater part of its volume, is the *mass public,* composed of opinion-holders who have neither the opportunity nor the inclination to participate in the opinion-making process. Members of the mass public, in other words, fall at the lower end of both the accessibility and the motivation-information scales. The middle stratum, located near the top of the pyramid, is the *attentive public,* consisting of opinion-holders who are inclined to participate but lack the access or opportunity to do so. Attentive opinion-holders are thus those who fall at the lower end of the accessibility scale and the upper end of the motivation-information scale. At the very tip of the pyramid is the *opinion-making public,* composed of those who are, as indicated, located above the zero point on both scales.[3]

The notion of a stationary pyramid is perhaps a poor way of introducing behavioral differences among the three strata of the public. A more appropriate analogy is that of a gigantic theater, with a tense drama unfolding on the stage.* The mass public, occupying the many seats in the balcony, is so far removed from the scene of action that its members can hardly grasp the plot, much less hear all the lines or distinguish between the actors. Thus they may sit in stony silence or applaud impetuously, if not so vigorously as to shake the foundations of the theater. Usually, however, they get thoroughly bored and leave, declining as they go invitations to occupy the empty seats in the orchestra. The attentive public, on the other hand, is located in the few choice orchestra seats. Its members can not only hear every spoken line clearly, but can also see the facial expressions of the actors. Thus they become absorbed in the drama, applauding its high spots and disparaging its flaws. Indeed, their involvement is such that during the intermission they make their views known to

---

* Elmo Roper uses still another analogy, that of concentric circles, as a means of developing "the hypothesis that in so far as the flow of ideas is concerned, the entire American public can be stratified into six groups." Moving outward from the inner circle, Roper designates his six publics as the "Great Thinkers," the "Great Disciples," the "Great Disseminators," the "Lesser Disseminators," the "Participating Citizens," and the "Politically Inert" (*op. cit.,* and the Foreword, in Katz and Lazarsfeld, *op. cit.,* pp. xv-xix). The last two of Roper's categories are roughly the equivalent of the attentive and mass publics, while his two groups of disseminators approximate what we have called the opinion-making public. Our conceptualization is not so explicit about the two innermost circles of Roper's scheme, but the few persons to which they apply also come under our definition of opinion-makers.

any occupants of the balcony who may have wandered into the lobby. As for the members of the opinion-making public, they are the actors on the stage, performing their parts with gusto and intensity, not infrequently in an effort to upstage each other. Many are directing their performance at some specific portion of the orchestra audience. Others, those with especially strong vocal cords, try to make themselves heard as far as the balcony. All are keenly aware that the quality of their performance will greatly affect their bargaining power when they seek higher salaries or better parts in future productions.*

The Mass Public

Let us look more closely at the largest stratum. By almost any yardstick, the mass public includes a preponderant majority of the nation. Estimates of its size vary from 75 to 90 per cent of the adult population.[4] The mass public is uninformed about either specific foreign-policy issues or foreign affairs in general. Its members pay little, if any, attention to day-to-day developments in world politics. Being uninformed and without initiative, they lack structured opinions—that is, they are short of the cognitive and evaluative equipment which facilitates comprehension of the ideas and information that are flowing through the circulatory system. Thus their response to foreign-policy matters is less one of intellect and more one of emotion; less one of opinion and more one of mood, of generalized, superficial, and undisciplined feelings which easily fluctuate from one extreme to another—from tolerance to intoler-

* Anticipating distinctions we shall later make between national and local opinion-makers, and between multi-issue and single-issue opinion-makers, this analogy can be carried further by noting that some occupants of the orchestra seats are members of the show's road company and are attending the performance with a view to learning their parts.

ance, optimism to pessimism, idealism to cynicism, with-drawal to intervention.[5]

The most predominant mood of the mass public is, of course, indifference and passivity. Except for acute peace-or-war crises (and not always then), the mass public is usually unmoved by the course of world events. Few of its members are likely to have more than headline ac-quaintance with public discussions of foreign-policy issues or be willing to listen to more than truncated news broad-casts over radio and television. And even when contact is made with more substantive programs, the mass public "does not listen to the content of discussion but to its tone."[6] In its passive mood, the mass public resists the prodding of opinion-makers, who are not content to let a slumbering giant rest. Few members of the mass public are likely to be activated into the temporary role of ama-teur opinion-submitters. Even fewer are likely to be en-ticed into permanent membership in the attentive public. As a passive mass, in other words, the mass public lies virtually outside the opinion-policy relationship. Its only function is that of setting, through the potentiality of its more active moods, the outer limits within which decision-makers and opinion-makers feel constrained to operate and interact. Since these limits are very broad, and since the mood of passivity prevails most of the time, it is the more structured and informed opinions of the attentive and opin-ion-making publics that usually determine the context within which the opinion-policy relationship functions.

On the rare occasions when it does awaken from its slum-ber, the mass public, being no more informed than previ-ously, is impulsive, unstable, unreasoning, unpredictable, capable of suddenly shifting direction or of going in several contradictory directions at the same time. The nation's reac-tions to Russia's launching of the first earth satellite in October 1957, or to the advent of Red China's entry into the Korean War in November 1950, might be cited as recent examples of this type of aroused behavior on the part of the mass public. At such times, its members turn more frequently to opinion-submitting, either through their own amateur efforts or through more active support of their representatives in the opinion-making public. An air of uncertainty and intolerance is introduced into the "climate" of public opinion. The area of decision-making permissiveness is narrowed as the mass public moves closer to the center of the opinion-policy relationship. Instability and irrationality enter the policy-making process as both decision-makers and opinion-makers seek to cope with the changing moods and tempo of mass opinion. Hence it would seem that, given these conditions as the alternative to indifference, the prevalence of the mass public's passive mood introduces a factor of stability into the foreign policy-making process.

The respective consequences of the mass public's passive and active moods are amply illustrated by what has been called "attention groups." [7] These are unorganized segments of the mass public, such as ethnic minorities, which are normally passive and disinterested, but which acquire structure as an aroused group whenever an issue arises that directly affects their common interests—for example, the liberation of Eastern Europe. Their entrance into public debate is then sudden and impulsive, and confined exclusively to the single issue which provoked them. Their recommendations concern only that issue, unmodified by and irrespective of the requirements of any other policy considerations. Once the issue has subsided, these attention groups disband (in so far as foreign policy is concerned), returning to the status of unorganized and passive segments of the mass public. Their cumulative effect "can be understood in terms of the analogy of loaded pistols which are triggered off by special issues which bring generally inattentive and uninformed groups into a sudden impact on the policy-making process." [8]

Attention groups emphasize the heterogeneous composition of the mass public. They come into being because members of the mass public have a variety of political, economic, and social affiliations which can form the basis of temporary emergence from passivity. Some of these affiliations derive from organizational membership, as in a union, a trade association, or a religious club. Others are derived from reference group membership, as in a social class, an occupational field, or a religious denomination. The net result of both types of affiliation is a mass public of enormous diversity, of disparate and crisscrossing segments that have in common only a passivity and moodiness toward foreign-policy issues. Each affiliative segment, moreover, tends to have spokesmen in the opinion-making public, a linkage which, as will be seen, constitutes a major impersonal channel of communication in the circulatory system. In short, contrary to the impression conveyed by our reference to the mass public as an *it* that awakes or slumbers or feels or sets limits, neither most Americans nor their leaders are joined together in a grand and homogeneous organization that *does* things. By "mass public" we do not mean an identifiable actor; rather, the term and the action verbs associated with it are a shorthand method of describing the combined *effect* of unrelated actions or opinions (or inaction or nonopinion) which are undertaken or held by countless persons and groups that are ordinarily inattentive to international affairs.

Nor does our definition of the mass public contain an implicit explanation of its behavior. To say that the mass public includes those who have neither the inclination nor the opportunity to participate in the opinion-making process is not to say that the former characteristic is a consequence of the latter, or that members of the mass public are passive and moody because they lack a chance to be active participants in the public debate over foreign-policy issues. If this were the case, there would be no conceptual room for the empirical fact that some persons, the attentive public, *do* possess an interest in and structured opinions about such matters, despite a similar lack of access to the opinion-making process. The opportunity to participate through occupancy of certain leadership positions does, to be sure, foster an inclination to do so. If members of the mass public were to move into these opinion-making positions their passivity toward foreign affairs would probably change. But the holding of such a position is not necessarily prerequisite to an active interest in foreign policy, as the attentive public demonstrates. The definitions of the three publics, in short, are empirical and not causal. Obviously, the reasons for the passivity of most Americans are more complex than simply the scarcity of opportunities to join the ranks of opinion-makers.

The Attentive Public

As the foregoing implies, in some respects the attentive public closely resembles the mass public. It too is an unorganized cross section of the nation. Its members may have higher incomes and more formal education than those of the mass public, but, taken as a whole, they hardly represent a homogeneous stratum of American society. Indeed, being composed of individuals with structured opinions, the attentive public probably encompasses greater diversity of outlook than does the mass public with its unstructured moods. A second similarity between the two is, of course, one of definition: in neither case do members of these publics occupy leadership positions which provide their occupants with access to the impersonal channels of the communications system. As noted below, the role of the attentive public in the opinion-making process is highly significant, but it does not include participation in the opinion-making process itself.

Nevertheless, these similarities between the attentive and mass publics are far less important than the several ways in which they differ. One distinguishing feature of the attentive public is its size, which, though variously estimated, is small by almost any standard. Based on the

circulation figures of the "quality media," * the attentive
public is probably no larger than 10 per cent of the population, and possibly much smaller. Elmo Roper estimates
that this stratum, which he calls the "Participating Citizens," is composed of "as many as ten to twenty-five
million Americans." [9] Another observer suggests that the
attentive public may be constantly "increasing in size and
in discrimination" because the universities, the quality
media of communication, and the civic interest groups are
more effectively stimulating more persons to maintain an
interest in foreign affairs.[10] Whatever the trend, however,
in the foreseeable future the attentive public will remain
minute in comparison to the mass public.

A second and much more important difference between
the two publics is that members of the attentive public
are more inclined to participate in the opinion-making
process even though they have no opportunity to do so.
Being continuously interested in foreign-policy matters,
they are aware of the major issues and well informed with
respect to them. Consequently the opinions which they internalize have structure and depth. While they too may
occasionally respond to crises in an impetuous and moody
way, members of the attentive public are not likely to
persist in such behavior for very long. Their high level
of interest and information serves to check the growth
and maintenance of moods. In terms of concrete action,
probably a substantial proportion of the attentive public
frequently writes to decision-makers or engages in other
forms of amateur opinion-submitting. Presumably it is
also comprised of persons who constitute the active membership (though not the leadership) of voluntary associations. Although members of the mass and attentive
publics may have their names side by side on associational

* These are the channels through which members of the
attentive public tend to acquire their opinions about foreign-
policy issues (see Chapter 6).

rosters, it is the latter who are more likely to attend meetings and otherwise support associational efforts and policies.

Of course, the factors which lead to attentiveness are no less complex or easy to explain than those which produce indifference and passivity. Here we shall have to content ourselves with the simple conclusion that permanent members of the attentive public, as distinguished from members of the mass public who are temporarily activated by the special interests of an attention group, find intellectual stimulation and satisfaction in matters pertaining to foreign policy. The behavioral consequences of this intellectual hobby amount to a crucial role for the attentive public in the opinion-making process. Not only does this public constitute one of the key links in the vertical channels of communication between the opinion-making and mass publics, but, more important, the attentive public serves as a critical audience for opinion-makers as they discuss and debate foreign-policy issues. Such an audience, alert to the intricacies of day-to-day policy situations, tends to offset the irrational impact of mass moods and to fill the vacuum which exists when indifference is the prevailing mood. Members of the attentive public provide, in effect, a forum in which foreign-policy controversy among opinion-makers can occur openly and in specific rather than superficial terms. Thus, as the stratum of society to which opinion-makers make special appeals for support, the attentive public introduces a more effective measure of democratic control into the opinion-policy relationship then does the mass public. If the latter sets the outer limits beyond which policy choices cannot be made, then the former can be said to determine the inner limits within which the opinion-policy relationship operates.

Chapter 5

THE OPINION-MAKERS

Some clarification of terms is required as we turn now to a closer examination of the opinion-making public. As previously noted, this uppermost stratum of the public has been designated in many different ways: as the elite, the effective public, the opinion leaders, and so on. At the risk of confounding rather than clarifying the situation, the designation "opinion-maker" has been introduced for several reasons. These do not include, however, a desire to avoid the value connotations that have become associated with existing designations. Lasswell is undoubtedly correct when he notes that judgmental overtones will inevitably be attached to "any new word introduced in place of elite . . . since whatever refers to a high position comes, by a process of generalization, to have normative connotations." [1] Nevertheless, the term "opinion-maker"

is offered in the belief that it is more precise and therefore
can more easily be made operational.

In the first place, all of the existing designations include
three or four types of behavior which, for our purposes,
are more appropriately considered as three or four separate
roles. Take, for example, this definition of the effective
public as comprising

> those individuals and groups who are the nation's opinion
> leaders because they strongly *influence,* as well as *articulate*
> and *represent,* the opinions of the mass public and because
> they have various types of access to the policy-making proc-
> ess and to policy makers.[2]

The words "influence," "articulate," and "represent" re-
spectively reflect what we have called opinion-circulating,
opinion-forming, and opinion-submitting. It is true, of
course, that often these three roles are performed simultaneously by the same person. Nevertheless—and this is
the main point—each role can be performed separately
without necessarily invoking or involving the other two.
Opinion-forming may be followed by opinion-circulating
in one situation, by opinion-submitting in another, and by
neither in still a third situation. Some members of this
uppermost stratum may never be active in more than one
of these roles, whereas others may be constantly shifting
back and forth among all three. Moreover, decision-makers
who shift roles illustrate a fourth type of behavior. Similarly, while there is considerable accuracy in the obser-
vation that he "who mobilizes the elites, mobilizes the
public," [3] such a conception also misleadingly implies
simultaneous performance of multiple roles. An elite which
has been mobilized for the purpose of forming opinions
may not at the same time engage in opinion-circulating
or opinion-submitting.

A second and closely related reason for eschewing these
other designations is that they all convey implications of
influence and consequence which do not necessarily inhere

in the functions performed by occupants of the designated positions. For example, while members of the "effective" public are accorded functions similar to those we attribute here to opinion-makers, such functions can be carried out with varying degrees of effectiveness or, indeed, with no effectiveness whatsoever. Likewise, to use the term "leader" or "leadership" in this context is to imply a followership which may not always accompany the opinion-making behavior. Since "the influential are the elite," [4] this latter term also tends to suggest consequences which extend beyond the processes of forming, circulating, and submitting opinions. This is not to say that the opinion-making public is regarded as ineffective or lacking influence. On the contrary, its members are presumed to constitute the leadership stratum of the society and to be more influential and effective than members of the attentive or mass publics. Such characteristics, however, are extrinsic rather than intrinsic to opinion-making activity. Their presence in any given opinion-making situation must be treated as problematic and established by empirical research rather than by conceptualization or its nomenclature.

Admittedly, the use of an unfamiliar designation does not guarantee avoidance of these conceptual difficulties, especially since the term "opinion-making" might also be equated with the presence of influence and the performance of a single role. It is hoped, however, that the very unfamiliarity of the new term will continually remind us that we are not assuming the prior existence of influence, and that the separate roles of opinion-forming and opinion-circulating are encompassed by our designation. Moreover, the term "opinion-making" easily lends itself to operationalization by drawing our attention to a specific form of behavior that can be observed, categorized, and measured. Indeed, opinion-making connotes behavior far more clearly and precisely than do any of the other designations. Whereas we can speak of opinion-makers as engaging in opinion-making, it is awkward to refer to members of the elite or effective publics as "eliting" or "effecting." Hopefully, this terminological orientation to action will also serve as a reminder that we cannot use our concepts as evidence of the empirical phenomena which they are intended to describe.

In order to develop a definition that will help us to identify and classify opinion-makers, let us return to the notion of an accessibility scale and view it as being composed of two dimensions which, when combined, differentiate four basic types of opinion-makers. One dimension is the geographic, which facilitates a distinction between national and local opinion-makers; the other is what might be called the functional dimension, which allows for a separation of multi- and single-issue opinion-makers. These two dimensions overlap, resulting in four main groupings: national multi-issue opinion-makers, national single-issue opinion-makers, local multi-issue opinion-makers, and local single-issue opinion-makers. The special characteristics of each of these groups are evident from a brief analysis of the general definition under which all of them are subsumed: the designation of "opinion-maker" is given to all members of the society who *occupy positions which enable them regularly to transmit, either locally or nationally, opinions about any issue to unknown persons outside of their occupational field or about more than one class of issues to unknown professional colleagues.*

In the order of their appearance, then, let us examine each of the key phrases in this generalized conception. In the sense that it is not the means by which opinion-makers are to be identified empirically, the phrase "occupy positions which enable" could have been omitted from the definition. The act of transmitting opinion serves as the basis for identifying opinion-makers and in no way is the definition intended to imply that an examination of specified occupational positions will lead to their identification. The latter procedure would be encumbered by all of the difficulties which attend the search for possessed qualities, and it would soon be clear that only by looking for those who transmit opinion through impersonal channels could we locate the positions which enable their occupants to behave as opinion-makers. Nevertheless, this phrase has been included in the definition so as to emphasize the central assumption (below) that the capacity to introduce opinions into the impersonal channels derives from the nature of certain positions in the society and the respect which they command, rather than from the qualities of their occupants.

The word "regularly" in this definition is intended to exclude persons whose access to the impersonal channels is limited to discontinuous types of action, such as writing letters to newspapers. Taken together, such letters may have important consequences; they may even come to the attention of decision-makers and affect their deliberations. Yet, for a variety of self-evident reasons, it seems unwise to designate the individual letter-writer as an opinion-maker if this is the only action by which he falls under the remainder of the definition. This is not to imply, however, that opinion-makers must continuously or frequently engage in the act of transmitting opinions. "Regularly" does not suggest even a minimum frequency of opinion-making behavior which opinion-makers must maintain. As long as periodicity marks their actions they may, like some authors, introduce ideas into the impersonal channels as infrequently as, say, every second or third year and still be regarded as opinion-makers.

The phrase "either locally or nationally" has of course been included in the definition to take into account the geographic dimension of accessibility. Since opinion-making capacities are acquired through the occupancy of certain positions or roles which command respect from groups of varying sizes and types, it follows that opinion-makers differ in the spatial range within which their opinions circulate. For example, the superintendent of a local school system will probably have access only to those impersonal channels of communication that traverse his community; a president of a state university will presumably be limited to those channels which are bounded by his state; and the head of a national education association will doubtless be able to transmit opinions to unknown persons outside of the state in which he resides. Obviously there are as many ways of operationalizing these spatial distinctions as there are geographic entities. Certain kinds of issues, such as racial discrimination or agricultural price supports, might well require a separate analysis of, say, neighborhood or regional opinion-makers. Here the distinction is confined to local and national opinion-makers because of the basic presumption, mentioned above, that little modification occurs in the structure, informational content, and judgmental direction of opinions about foreign-policy issues once they circulate beyond the ranks of national opinion-makers. It seems sufficient for our purposes, in other words, to define national opinion-makers as those who regularly transmit opinion to unknown persons living in other states, and to consider as local opinion-makers all those who regularly introduce opinions into impersonal channels that do not extend across state boundaries.[5]

The last two clauses of the overall definition deal with the same problem, namely, that the impersonal channels are subdivided along occupational as well as geographic lines, and that through them flow ideas and information of a technical or professional nature. The complexity of this problem can be illustrated by a closer look at the example of the school superintendent. Above it was estimated that he occupies a position which enjoys the respect of the community bounded by the school system, and that therefore he could probably introduce opinions about a variety of matters into its impersonal channels of communication. This is not, however, a complete estimate of his access to the communications system. For there is one class of opinions, those circumscribed by his professional expertise, which he can regularly transmit to unknown persons outside of his community and outside of the state in which he resides. Through professional journals and associational magazines, for instance, he can communicate his ideas about such matters as teachers' salaries and curriculum revision to other school superintendents with whom he is not acquainted. Does this mean that he and all those who write for professional journals and associational magazines should be classified as national opinion-makers? Or, to cite an even more pointed example, should the opinion-making designation be applied to the bacteriologist who frequently disseminates research findings in professional journals and who, unlike the school superintendent, is not so well known in his community as to be able to circulate opinions on other than bacteriological matters? Indeed, should such a specialist be considered an opinion-maker even at the local level?

In large part, it seems appropriate to answer questions of this sort in the negative. After all, we are concerned here with the communications system that underlies the opinion-policy relationship, so that our general definition should not be so broad as to encompass technical information and ideas which circulate within an occupational field and which pertain to those strictly professional matters that constitute the special expertise of its members. Our task, in other words, is not to account for all the opinions introduced into impersonal channels, but only for those which are relevant to the issues that activate the opinion-policy relationship. Accordingly, it seemed appropriate to add to the general definition the requirement that opinion-makers be able to transmit opinions about "any issue to unknown persons outside their occupational field."

But this blanket exclusion from the opinion-making public of those who transmit opinions to professional colleagues goes too far. Note needs to be taken of two important circumstances in which the communicative activities of occupational specialists are highly relevant to the opinion-policy relationship. Consider, for example, the labor leader who reviews the state of Soviet-American relations in the pages of his union's newspaper. While his opinions may circulate only among union members, surely he has participated in the opinion-making process in foreign policy. Presumably the same can be said of the head of a voluntary association or of the editor of its monthly magazine, who may be responsible for a page of commentary in each issue that allows or requires him to express opinions about questions which are related only indirectly, if at all, to the common concerns of the association's membership. Conceivably even the nation's leading bacteriologist is so widely respected within his field that he can use the pages of bacteriological journals as a means of circulating ideas and information about a variety of issues that have no direct bearing upon the professional interests of his unknown readers. There are, in short, at least a few leaders in every occupational field who, either because of their professional eminence or their associational responsibilities, are able regularly to introduce into the impersonal channels of their field opinions about matters that fall outside of their expertise. Hence it is necessary to include in the general definition those who transmit opinions about "more than one class of issues to unknown professional colleagues."

Although not so explicit in the definition, there is a second circumstance in which the occupational specialist may become an opinion-maker, namely, when an issue which activates the opinion-policy relationship embraces matters that fall within his expertise. For under these conditions his professional opinions are sought, thereby giving him access to impersonal channels outside of his field. If, for example, he is a school superintendent, and Russian technological developments foster the issue of how the science training of American youth can be improved, then his articles on teachers' salaries and curricular revision may be dug out of the journals of educational administration, quoted, and reprinted. He may even be asked to write articles for national magazines or appear on nationwide television programs, thus expanding his opinion-making activity beyond the local level. Moreover, if for some reason his local community has not previously accorded him access to its impersonal channels, certainly the emergence of the science-training issue would have such a consequence. By the same token, even the bacteriologist may become an opinion-maker at a time when an issue such as germ warfare is under public discussion. In fact, it seems likely that each occupational field encompasses one or another matter that may be potentially related to an issue which activates the opinion-policy relationship. And surely the reverse also obtains, namely, that every issue which precipitates this relationship evokes the expertise of some specialized field. In general, of course, the specialist has opinion-making status only for the one class of issues circumscribed by his professional competence, and he loses this status whenever the issues that focus attention upon him abate and his opinions are again relegated to the journals or other publications within his field.

It follows, therefore, that the membership of the opinion-making public is not fixed. As the issues that activate the opinion-policy relationship change, so do the number and kind of occupational experts who introduce opinions into the communications system. Stated differently, at both national and local levels the opinion-making public is composed of a core of persons who can regularly transmit opinions about many issues, and of an ever-changing group of specialists whose access is limited to matters encompassed by their expertise. The latter group shall henceforth be designated as *single-issue opinion-makers*[6] and the former as *multi-issue opinion-makers.*

The politician and the newspaper editor are clear-cut examples of multi-issue opinion-makers. Both are expected to have views about every controversy that concerns their constituents or their readers, and both do in fact circulate opinions about a wide variety of unrelated issues. But this is not to say that multi-issue opinion-makers are those whose positions enable them to disseminate ideas about all or most of the questions under public discussion. Some may have a more restricted access to the communications system. The head of a national religious organization, for example, might transmit opinions about educational issues as well as about those involving church-state relations. He might even be able to circulate his views on a number of foreign-policy questions. In all likelihood, however, his opinion-making activity will not embrace such issues as the parity formula for agricultural commodities or the monetary policies of the Federal Reserve Board. Similarly, geographic factors may limit the access of a multi-issue opinion-maker. A local politician, for example, may transmit opinions about sewage, highway, budgetary, and other community-wide problems, but have little or no opportunity or inclination to circulate his ideas on disarmament, foreign aid, summit diplomacy, and other international questions.

Multi-issue opinion-makers, in short, are characterized by an ability to engage in opinion-making activity that exceeds the scope of their professional competence, rather than by unlimited access to the impersonal channels. Strictly speaking, a person who regularly transmits opinions about as few as two classes of issues is considered a multi-issue opinion-maker. Of course, once an opinion-maker exceeds the scope of his professional competence, his opinion-making capacities are likely to extend to more than two sets of issues. It is for this reason that categorization has not been carried beyond the distinction between single- and multi-issue opinion-makers.

Precise definitions of the four main groups that comprise the opinion-making public logically emerge from the foregoing discussion. *National multi-issue opinion-makers* are those who can regularly transmit opinions about more than one class of issues to unknown persons living in other states. United States Senators or syndicated columnists, for example, would doubtless be subsumed by this definition, as would the activities of those who occupied such eminent positions as the presidency of Harvard University or the board chairmanship of the General Motors Corporation. *Local multi-issue opinion-makers* are those who regularly transmit opinions about more than one class of issues to unknown persons within their states. City mayors, editors of weekly newspapers, presidents of state universities, and owners of local factories would fall under this classification. *National single-issue opinion-makers* are those who regularly transmit opinions about only one class of issues to unknown persons outside of their state and their occupational field. This definition would apply to the Harvard professor of astronomy, or the General Motors engineer in charge of missile projects, who are invited to participate in a nation-wide television or radio program when the issue of, say, space exploration is under discussion. Finally, *local single-issue opinion-makers* are those who regularly transmit opinions about only one class of issues to unknown persons within their states and outside of their occupational fields. This definition would be applicable to the professor of astronomy at a state university and the head of a small company that manufactures missile nosecones, who are called upon to address local clubs on the subject of exploring outer space.*

* It should be noted that none of these definitions is complete, and that they all require further elaboration if they are to be applied to empirical data. As they stand, only the geographic dimension has been rendered operational; that is, any observer could distinguish a local opinion-maker from a national one by determining whether his opinions were transmitted beyond state boundaries. Differentiation between multi- and single-issue opinion-makers, however, requires precise formulation of the boundaries of an "issue." Similarly, the criteria for identifying and classifying "occupational fields" and the act of "regularly transmitting opinions" have to be specified if empirical use is to be made of these definitions. Since dif-

Viewed from the perspective of all the issues which activate the opinion-policy relationship at any one time, certain forms of dual membership in the opinion-making public appear to be possible. The simplest form is that of the national multi-issue opinion-maker, who, by virtue of his national prominence, also has access to the communications system of his local community. Equally obvious is the single-issue opinion-maker who can circulate his specialized opinions at both the national and local levels. Somewhat more complex is the case of the local multi-issue opinion-maker who fills a national single-issue role with respect to those matters that are circumscribed by his professional competence. This form of dual membership is exemplified by the aforementioned school superintendent, whose position enables him to circulate opinions on many issues at the local level and whose opinion-making capacities are geographically extended whenever the issue of science training comes into being on a national scale. Indeed, it is not unlikely that many local multi-issue opinion-makers acquire extensive access to the local communications system through performing as single-issue opinion-makers at the national level. Such a process is presumably inherent in what is regarded as a central function of the mass media, namely, that of status conferral.[7] Both the process and the function can be illustrated by recurring to the hypothetical bacteriologist noted above. Let us assume that he is a local single-issue opinion-maker, or perhaps simply an opinion-holder, when the issue of germ warfare activates the opinion-policy relationship. Suppose the development of the issue leads to his being called upon to present his expert views to a Congressional committee that is hearing testimony in a nationally televised public session. To point up the dynamics of the process, let us further presume that he becomes involved in a prolonged alterca-

---

ferent research situations may involve different issues, fields, and actions, these terms have not been defined at this point.

tion with a Senator over the prospects of bateriological warfare. The publicity and acclaim resulting from such an incident may so enhance the bacteriologist's prominence in the local community as to afford him access to its impersonal channels on matters far removed from the germ-warfare issue. Moreover, even if his place in the national spotlight declines as the issue wanes, his status back home may not diminish, so that the transition from single- to multi-issue opinion-maker is thus made permanent.*

Other possible combinations of dual membership are suggested by the possibility that, on certain issues, some opinion-makers may not have any access to the impersonal channels. Under these circumstances, they become opinion-holders in either the mass or the attentive publics. Presumably they will usually join the ranks of the attentive public whenever they are not able to engage in opinion-making. Such a presumption seems reasonable on the grounds that positions which provide access to the impersonal channels on any issue involve responsibilities which encourage the holders of these positions to concern themselves about other issues under public discussion. On the other hand, it is at least theoretically possible that some persons may shift back and forth between the opinion-making and mass publics as their location on the accessibility scale fluctuates from issue to issue. Conceivably some opinion-makers are interested only in those matters encompassed by their professional competence and thus they are members of the mass public whenever their expertise does not afford them access to the impersonal channels at either the local or national level.

While dual membership of this kind is most likely in the case of single-issue opinion-makers, it is not entirely in-

* Such a transition could, of course, also occur at the national level, as is strikingly illustrated by the opinion-making activities of Mr. Joseph N. Welch subsequent to his nationally televised clash with Senator Joseph R. McCarthy, in the so-called Army-McCarthy hearings of June 1954.

conceivable that certain types of multi-issue opinion-makers might also be members of the mass public. Local politicians, for example, may not only lack access to the impersonal channels of their community on questions of foreign policy (except possibly in presidential election years), but they may also be so preoccupied with highway, sewage, tax, and other local problems that they pay no attention to world affairs. Indeed, this example suggests that membership in all three publics is theoretically possible. Some local politicians may be members of the opinion-making public with respect to local issues, of the attentive public with respect to national issues of domestic policy (e.g., the federal highway program), and of the mass public with respect to foreign-policy issues.

The foregoing analysis of the shifting composition of the opinion-making public suggests the probability that opinion-making activity takes place primarily at the national level on issues relating to foreign policy and at all levels on issues relating to domestic policy. As implied in the example of local politicians, many local opinion-makers acquire access to the impersonal channels because their positions involve responsibility for the immediate needs of their community. Thus their opinions on the course of world affairs are not sought by the community and on such matters they must perforce revert to the role of opinion-holders. Editors of community newspapers, unable to give extensive coverage to foreign news in their weekly editions, provide another good illustration of local opinion-makers who ordinarily have no access to the impersonal channels on questions of foreign policy. On the other hand, the connection between the community's welfare and domestic policy is far more direct, so that local opinion-makers may well be as active in these areas as are their colleagues at the national level. It follows that the pattern of opinion circulation is likely to be a *two-step flow* with respect to foreign-policy issues and a *three-step flow* with respect to domestic-policy issues. That is, in both instances opinions are likely to be introduced into impersonal channels by national opinion-makers, and then passed on through personal channels by opinion leaders; but in the case of domestic issues, the circulation of these opinions is likely to be sustained by local opinion-makers who reintroduce them into the impersonal channels of the community as well as by opinion leaders who are active in face-to-face situations.

Before we categorize the opinion-making public any further, let us briefly examine how and why relatively few persons in the society acquire access to the impersonal channels. Thus far we have merely alluded to the notion that opinion-making capacities derive from the nature of certain leadership positions or roles. Now it is appropriate to elaborate upon the sources of membership in the opinion-making public. Our basic assumption is that all types of opinion-makers acquire access to the impersonal channels in either of two ways: by *ascription* or by *achievement*. The former process is predominant. Access to the communications system is ascribed in the sense that most opinion-makers hold positions of prominence in organizations which are so highly respected by the local or national community that they are called upon to circulate their opinions to other than face-to-face acquaintances. Ascribed opinion-making capacities, in other words, are attached to occupational roles and do not derive from special talents possessed by opinion-makers. The ascribed capacities are present in the role rather than in the individual. For example, the president of a large university and the executive officer of a large corporation have access to the impersonal channels of communication regardless of whether they seek or utilize outlets for their opinions. Newspapers cover their public activities, groups request them to give speeches, radio and television producers ask them to appear on programs, and so on. Thus, although running a university and managing a corporation constitute the formal requirements of their occupational roles, informally these men are obliged to devote time to handling opportunities to introduce opinions into the communications system. It is the informal nature of these obligations which leads us to speak of opinion-making capacities as "attached" to an occupational role, rather than as inherent in the role.*

But it might be argued that a man cannot become president of a university or board chairman of a corporation unless he has special talents. Surely opinion-makers must be particularly gifted in order to occupy the leadership positions to which opinion-making capacities are attached. How, then, can it be said that most opinion-makers acquire their access to the impersonal channels through ascription rather than achievement? The answer to this question involves a subtle distinction that further illustrates the ascribed nature of most opinion-making capacities: while talent and a record of achievement are undoubtedly essential to promotion to leadership positions in organizations that command respect, ordinarily it is the occupancy of the positions that provides access to the impersonal channels, rather than the skills or accomplishments which led to occupancy.

The only exception to this ascriptive manner of becoming an opinion-maker concerns those who, like artists, scholars, and sports stars, are recognized and respected because of accomplishments attained through individual effort outside of an organizational framework. Whenever local or national prominence is acquired in this way, opinion-making capacities can be said to have been achieved rather than ascribed. This distinction can also be depicted in terms of the loss of access to the impersonal

* It should be noted, however, that opinion-making capacities are formally prescribed aspects of a few specific types of occupational roles. Those who operate the mass media are the most obvious example of opinion-makers who must circulate opinions to unknown persons in order to perform their jobs.

channels. Opinion-makers who acquire their access through ascription will usually lose it by resigning from their occupational positions, whereas access acquired through personal achievement cannot be lost in such an abrupt fashion. Prolonged inactivity might result in the loss of achieved opinion-making capacities, but no single action such as resignation or retirement could bring this about.

The notion that access to the communications system derives mainly from organizational positions suggests a third dimension of the accessibility scale, one which might be called the occupational dimension and which necessitates further subcategorization of the opinion-making public. That is, not only are national, local, single-issue, and multi-issue opinion-makers likely to behave in different ways, but presumably those with similar types of access derived from similar kinds of occupational roles will also engage in distinctive forms of opinion-making activity. Indeed, as previously indicated, occupational factors are important determinants of both the geographic scope and the issue range within which opinion-makers can circulate their views. Given the multitude of pursuits in which men engage, however, classification of opinion-makers along occupational lines can be an endless task.[8] Innumerable subcategories could be developed to account for the many kinds of occupational specialists who become single-issue opinion-makers as a result of the many kinds of issues that activate the opinion-policy relationship. Here the problem of encyclopedism has been avoided by subsuming all types of occupational access under these four main headings: governmental, associational, institutional, and individual.[9] To be sure, this fourfold breakdown, when combined with the geographic and functional dimensions of the accessibility scale, yields sixteen basic types of opinion-makers. But, while this scheme may be somewhat unwieldy, each of the sixteen categories does have important and distinctive features, as the examples in this typology suggest:

Occupational Type	*National Multi-issue Opinion-Makers*	*National Single-issue Opinion-Makers*	*Local Multi-issue Opinion-Makers*	*Local Single-issue Opinion-Makers*
Governmental opinion-makers	A United States Senator	Assistant Secretary of State for European Affairs	City mayor	Chief customs officer of a port city
Associational opinion-makers	National commander of the American Legion	President of the Foreign Policy Association	Commander of a city's American Legion post	Head of a county's refugee organization
Institutional opinion-makers	Chairman of the board of the General Motors Corporation	Head of a missile-manufacturing company	President of a city's leading bank	Partner in a coffee-importing firm
Individual opinion-makers	Syndicated columnist	The nation's leading demographer	Prominent author in the community	Professor of Asiatic Affairs at a near-by college

Leaving aside the geographic and functional dimensions of the accessibility scale, let us now examine the four types of occupational access more closely.

Governmental Opinion-Makers

Governmental access to the impersonal channels accrues to those who occupy elected, appointed, or career positions in any branch of government at the federal, state, or local levels. But, of course, not every government official can become an opinion-maker. Rather, access is available only to those whose positions provide sufficient prestige and authority to permit them to introduce opinions into the communications system. This means that, in matters of foreign policy, governmental opinion-makers will normally be federal officials, although occasionally some officers of state and local governments may be able to shift into an opinion-making role. On particular issues such officials as, say, state governors or city mayors can make a more substantial contribution to the opinion-making process than is generally recognized.* The limitations on their activities in this area, however, reflect the important point that governmental opinion-makers are not necessarily foreign-policy decision-makers. State and local officials may have access to the opinion-making process, but their duties are usually far removed from the decision-making process. Given exclusive jurisdiction over foreign affairs, only officials at the federal level are in a position to shift back and forth between opinion-making and decision-making roles. Not all federal officials, however, can make this shift. Some may occupy junior decision-making positions that do not provide access to the communications system. Others may have high rank and opinion-making access, but lack the capacity to become foreign-policy decision-makers because their responsibilities pertain primarily to domestic matters. Indeed, their lack of access to the decision-making process may lead them to turn to opinion-making as a method of impressing their views upon their colleagues who operate in the foreign affairs field.

Of course, the main governmental opinion-makers are the federal officials who are responsible for the formulation and conduct of foreign policy (such as members of Congress on the relevant committees or top administrators in the pertinent executive agencies) and who are therefore able to shift between decision-making and opinion-making roles. As previously indicated, such officials frequently participate in the opinion-making process chiefly to enhance

---

* Note, for example, the activities of New York City's Mayor Robert F. Wagner, in January 1957, and of Detroit's Mayor Louis J. Miriani, in June 1959, when it was proposed that King Ibn Saud of Saudi Arabia and Deputy Premier Frol R. Kozlov of the USSR visit their respective cities as part of a good will tour of the United States.

their efforts as decision-makers. The manner and extent of their opinion-making activity varies widely. Some shift from the decision-making role more readily than others; some direct their appeals at the mass public; others try to reach the attentive public; still others focus upon communicating with fellow members of the opinion-making public. Since many of these differences stem from distinctions between the legislative, executive, and judicial branches, particular empirical situations would doubtless require further subcategorization of governmental opinion-makers.

Associational Opinion-Makers

Associational access to the opinion-making process is held by those who occupy either elected or high staff positions in any of the innumerable national, regional, or local voluntary associations that are dispersed so widely throughout American society.[10] Associational opinion-makers derive their access to communications from the fact that they speak, not as individuals, but as representatives of groups of opinion-holders who are organized around at least one common characteristic or interest.

It follows that associational opinion-makers tend also to be professional opinion-submitters who, as noted, often turn to opinion-making in order to increase the effectiveness of their submissions. They usually do so by introducing opinions into the communications system of their associations and, as previously implied, in this capacity they will probably be able to circulate their views on a variety of issues. Some associational opinion-makers may also try to mobilize segments of the larger society in support of their associational goals. Under these circumstances, their access may be reduced to those issues circumscribed by the interests which their associations are designed to serve and which they are supposed to represent. Presumably multi-issue access to the impersonal channels of the larger society accrues only to those associational opinion-makers who hold positions in large and well-established organizations. In short, if inclined to do so, most associational opinion-makers could probably circulate opinions about foreign-policy issues to their membership, but similar activity directed to nonmembers can only be undertaken by those who represent prominent organizations or ones with special interests in foreign affairs.

Associational opinion-makers may be classified in a number of different ways: (1) by the purity of their motives; (2) by the segments of society which they represent; (3) by the size of their associations; (4) by the number and kind of political issues with which they are concerned.[11] For our purposes, it is useful to subcategorize them under two major headings, each of which is further subdivided according to occupational classifications. The major distinction is between those who serve and represent *special-interest* associations and those who are affiliated with *civic-interest* associations. The former type are dedicated to the interests which its members have in common and which constitute the basis for their particular associational existence, whereas the latter type are primarily oriented toward the interests of society as a whole. Special-interest opinion-makers can be further subdivided in terms of their field of interest: agriculture, business, labor, veterans, and so on. Civic-interest opinion-makers can be subdivided either in terms of their association's membership basis (such as women's groups) or in terms of the aspects of the larger society with which they are concerned (such as foreign-policy groups or health and welfare organizations). The exact breakdown of each type will depend upon the requirements of particular empirical situations.

Associations having both special and civic interests are classified according to whether or not the latter are articulated in terms of the former. For example, while certain large business or labor associations may concern themselves with a number of foreign-policy issues pertaining to the welfare of the larger society, they are nevertheless considered special-interest associations because their concern is normally based on the question of how such issues will affect the interests of business or labor. Contrariwise, although religious associations are no less quick to protect their own interests when these are threatened, they are classified as civic-interest associations because ordinarily they also have humanitarian or reform motives that lead to a consistent concern about many foreign-policy issues which have no direct relation to matters of religion. Of course, where it is not clear which type of motive takes precedence in an association, this general distinction becomes somewhat arbitrary.

At this point it should be noted that the distinction between civic- and special-interest associations does not derive from a value judgment that the altruistic motives of the former are commendable, while those of the latter are selfish and undesirable. Rather it is intended to differentiate significant differences in behavior which appear to be a function of these two variables. Thus, if civic-interest associations are concerned with foreign-policy issues at all, their activities are frequently organized around international questions, whereas special-interest associations focus only upon those issues which affect their immediate interests. In other words, civic-interest associations tend to be composed of permanent members of the attentive public, while special-interest associations tend to include those segments of the mass public that temporarily and impulsively join the attentive public via the aforementioned route of attention groups. The consequence of this difference for the two types of associational opinion-makers is self-evident. To be sure, both types turn to opinion-making in an effort to activate or serve their associations. But they do so in very different ways. The civic-interest opinion-maker is continuously active in the opinion-making process, thereby providing the basis for a steady and structured attentiveness to foreign affairs on the part of those he represents. On the other hand, the special-interest opinion-maker participates in the process sporadically and spasmodically, depending on whether or not a particular foreign-policy issue impinges upon the interests of his association. If and when his association is affected, he translates the issue into opinions which are narrowly structured reflections of his association's needs and wants. Thus he energizes his membership into sudden bursts of activity, rather than providing it with the basis for a permanent emergence from passivity.

A third type of voluntary association, not mentioned before, cuts across this distinction between special and civic interests in such a way as to make classification along these lines impossible and to necessitate a third major subcategory of associational opinion-makers. We have in mind the political party and those who occupy its high elective or staff positions at the national, state, or local levels—that is, the politicians, whom we shall designate as political opinion-makers. The Democratic and Republican parties are by far the largest voluntary associations in the country. Among their members are civic- and special-interest opinion-makers as well as all other types. This includes governmental opinion-makers, many of whom are high-ranking party officials who would normally be designated as political opinion-makers if this term were not reserved for politicians who hold no governmental position. Obviously the common associational membership of political and governmental opinion-makers greatly facilitates the opinion-submitting tasks of the former and the opinion-making efforts of the latter.

Despite their differences, associational opinion-makers share one quality which presumably sets them apart from other members of the opinion-making public. Because their positions require them to represent and serve the interests of their membership, a task which involves skillful juggling of various conflicting and overlapping expectations, associational opinion-makers tend to become specialists in the techniques of developing a consensus (or the appearance thereof). They become expert at sponsoring events and distributing literature, writing press releases, keeping open many different channels of communication, harmonizing organizational differences, and fashioning majorities where previously none existed. These attributes may seem to equate the associational opinion-maker with the public-relations specialist, but although the associational opinion-maker does develop a talent for public relations and a knowledge of when and how to use what channels of communication for particular purposes, he also develops other abilities besides those which mark the publicity agent. Not only must he be skilled in the use of various channels of communication, but he must also acquire what may be called "organizational know-how"—that is, the faculty of using the structure and resources of an organization for a particular set of purposes.

Organizational know-how in this sense is a talent which perhaps only those in representational work acquire. To be sure, many positions require their occupants to direct organizations. As will be seen, most institutional opinion-makers manage or administer organizations and, in the performance of this task, are required to maximize organizational output. Only associational executives, however, are constantly engaged in mobilizing the resources of an organization *behind a point of view*. In this sense, associational opinion-makers may be regarded as professional participants in the opinion-making process. Thus, while they may reach fewer opinion-holders than other types of opinion-makers, and may even be less influential in molding opinions than some of their colleagues, their behavior needs to be separately examined in view of the resources at their disposal and the specialized talents they command.

Institutional Opinion-Makers

Persons who hold high positions in organizations which form a basic institution of American society are regarded as institutional opinion-makers. Businessmen, clergymen, educators, lawyers, and publishers would, for example, be classified in this category. Their access to the opinion-making process derives from the prestige attached to their organizational positions—a prestige which, as previously indicated, commands respect in their community and thus enables them to circulate opinions through its impersonal channels. Affiliated with such diverse organizations as the corporation, church, school, and newspaper, institutional opinion-makers commonly hold formal positions of authority to which is added the informal authority that stems from long, even permanent, tenure in office. Moreover, unlike associational opinion-makers, whose opinions circulate mainly within their associations, institutional opinion-makers are among the "notables" of their community, so that their opinions are likely to circulate beyond the organizations with which they are affiliated. A university president, for instance, has access to a larger audience than the students and faculty of the university he heads. In fact, the organization with which they are affiliated constitutes a very small channel in the communications system to which institutional opinion-makers have access.

As suggested above, institutional opinion-makers may be subdivided in terms of such varied fields as communications, education, religion, business, and law.[12] In turn, each of these categories could be broken down into smaller units, such as types of business firms, educational levels or fields, religious denominations, and so on. Of the major types of institutional opinion-makers, the first requires special emphasis and elaboration. Leaders in the communications field enjoy advantages which do not accrue to other institutional opinion-makers, nor, for that matter, to governmental, associational, and individual opinion-makers. Communications opinion-makers are not only located astride the major impersonal channels of communication, but they also command access to most of them by virtue of owning or operating the mass media. They are the journalists, editors, publishers, commentators, columnists, and television and movie producers who circulate opinions, either their own or those of other opinion-makers, far and wide to all strata of the public. To be sure, the mass media are not the only channels of impersonal communication, as we shall shortly indicate; but they are considerably more extensive than any of the others, and they are also the main channels through which the opinions of other opinion-makers circulate. Indeed, much of the "interaction" between opinion-makers of all types takes place at long range through the mass media, a fact which indicates the large extent to which the opinion-making process is itself a function of the activities of these institutional opinion-makers in the communications field.

To revert briefly to our earlier analogy with the theater, communications opinion-makers operate the theater in which the opinion-making drama unfolds. They are in a position to draw the curtain, change the scenery, redirect the spotlights, and control the amplifying system. Other opinion-makers must either be content with a small, off-Broadway channel, or they must act with sufficient drama to gain access to the well-equipped stage of the playhouse which the communications opinion-makers run in the very heart of the theater district. In short, other opinion-makers, as well as the mass and attentive publics, are very much dependent upon the communications opinion-makers for their knowledge of what transpires in foreign affairs and of how other types of opinion-makers size up and judge the prevailing issues.

Emphasis upon the importance of communications opinion-makers is not intended to imply a lack of differentiation among businessmen, clergymen, educators, or lawyers. Presumably each of these groups has different kinds and degrees of access to opinion-making, which in turn lead to different types of opinion-making behavior. In general, for example, businessmen probably have access to fewer vertical channels of communication than, say, educators, so that the latter may circulate their opinions more widely than the former to the attentive and mass publics. On the other hand, businessmen may have more extensive ties with other members of the opinion-making public than do educators, with the result that their opinions may circulate more widely through horizontal channels than do those of educational leaders. Moreover, varied interests within each group of institutional opinion-makers may result in important behavioral differences. Conceivably, for instance, executives of large corporations and small businessmen may vary greatly in terms of the kind of foreign-policy issues with which they become concerned.

Nor is this to imply that every occupant of an institutional position is a national opinion-maker. Some businessmen, clergymen, educators, and lawyers are too remote from the opinion-making process to have any access to it at all. Others have perhaps only local or single-issue access. For example, while a corporation lawyer may be a national opinion-maker, his small-town colleague may not even have access to the local communications system. Similarly, a college teacher probably has more access than an elementary school teacher, a bishop more than a minister, and so on. Obviously it is impossible to draw a hard-and-fast line between those who are opinion-makers and those who are not. It can only be said that the higher a position is in an organization, and the wider the geographic or functional scope of the organization, the greater the likelihood that the position's holder will have membership in the opinion-making public.

It should also be noted that occupancy of more than one position provides certain persons both institutional and associational access to opinion-making. This occurs when a voluntary association (such as a trade association) elects to a position of authority someone who already holds a top post in a member organization (namely, some business firm). Similarly, multiple access accrues to the corporation executive who is elected to the presidency of the National Association of Manufacturers, or to the university president who is chosen for the chairmanship of the Association of Land Grant Colleges. Although multiple access to the opinion-making process complicates the analyst's task, usually it is possible to determine which type of access an opinion-maker is employing. If he acts in his associational capacity, which means that he will be representing more than his own organization, then he will probably introduce his opinions by saying that he speaks *for*—for the N.A.M. or for its membership. If, on the other hand, he is acting in his institutional capacity, which does not involve a representational orientation, then he will speak *as*—as a businessman or as head of a corporation. This distinction between "for" and "as" is especially useful in classifying certain groups, especially labor unions, which are on the borderline between voluntary associations and institutional organizations. Although unions could easily be placed in the latter category, here labor leaders are regarded as associational opinion-makers on the grounds that they are more likely to speak *for* labor or *for* their members than *as* labor leaders or *as* presidents of their unions.

Individual Opinion-Makers

Another type of opinion-maker is one who possesses what might, for want of a better term, be called individual access to the opinion-making process. Persons so classified have access to the impersonal channels of the communications system not because they occupy high positions in organizational structures, but because of some personal quality or achievement. Inherited wealth or family background, for example, may lead to such high social standing that membership in the opinion-making public is acquired apart from the occupancy of governmental, associational, or institutional positions. Artists and celebrities in the entertainment world are other examples of individual opinion-makers, as are novelists, intellectuals, and scientists. So occasionally are the widows, wives, and children of prominent persons. And so, most importantly, are persons who have retired from governmental, associational, or institutional positions, but who maintain access to opinion-making by virtue of their past achievements. To cite the most obvious example, a former president of the United States has considerable access to the communications system even if the only position he occupies after leaving the White House is that of a citizen from Independence or a gentleman farmer from Gettysburg. Indeed, probably the largest number of individual opinion-makers are those who carry into retirement a previously acquired positional prominence.

From the above it can be seen that individual opinion-makers are not easy to classify. In the first place, their qualities and achievements are so varied that further subdivision of their ranks would probably lead to an unmanageable number of subcategories. Nor is it easy to generalize about the degree of individual prominence which results in access to the impersonal channels of communication. Here again empirical evidence of actual participation in the opinion-making process is a better guide to classification than any general rule that may be devised. Similarly, it is not always clear whether an opinion-maker has acquired access through personal attainment or positional status. For example, should Henry A. Kissinger be classified as an individual or an institutional opinion-maker? Did he become a member of the opinion-making public because his book, *Nuclear Weapons and Foreign Policy*,[13] was the result of independent intellectual achievement or because it was written in compliance with the requirements of an organizational research position? These questions indicate that individual access is relative and that at the points where it overlaps with positional access arbitrary rules of classification have to be employed. Despite these complications, however, the category of individual opinion-maker is obviously needed to account for the welter of opinions which enter the circulatory system unaccompanied by the prestige of organizational position.

Although more crude and overlapping than definitive and exclusive, this multifold subcategorization of opinion-makers has the virtue of emphasizing a primary character-istic of the opinion-making public: its diversity and frag-mentariness. At the most, opinion-makers comprise 1 or 2 per cent of the population, and at least one observer puts their number at no more than 50,000 persons.[14] However, although few in number, opinion-makers by no means com-prise a homogeneous or organized group. The formulation of precise categories for analytic purposes suggests an or-derliness and organization of the opinion-making public which does not in fact exist. Rather, its members are almost infinitely varied in their relationships to equally varied fol-lowings, in their mode of forming and circulating opinions, in their willingness to utilize the opinion-making access available to them, in their familiarity with foreign affairs, and in their attitudes toward issues of foreign policy. This last kind of variation is perhaps the most consequential of all. As Almond has pointed out, heterogeneity rather than uniformity characterizes the ideology of the opinion-mak-ing public.[15] Each of its multitudinous segments has its own conception of what the aims and techniques of American foreign policy ought to be. There are few issues on which widespread or general agreement exists among members of the opinion-making public. The impersonal and personal channels of communication are filled not with a few main currents of opinion, but with countless eddies, each swirling in its own undertow.

Ideological autonomy in the opinion-forming process, moreover, is coupled with functional autonomy in the opinion-circulating process. Each segment of the opinion-making public is, relatively speaking, able to conduct its activities independently of the actions or attitudes of any other segment. Opinion-makers are variously linked with the attentive and mass publics, so that they are not impelled by a mutual interdependence to develop a consensus on matters of foreign policy or to coordinate their opinion-making efforts. To be sure, opinion-makers are not entirely isolated from one another. Communication does occur between them as varying segments interact with each other. The functional autonomy of opinion-makers, however, casts their interaction into a competitive rather than a cooperative mold. Indeed, it may even be that much of what appears to be interaction among opinion-makers is not interaction at all—rather it is construed as such by the observer who imposes structure upon separate, autonomous endeavors undertaken contemporaneously by unrelated opinion-makers.

Regardless of whether it is superimposed from without or self-generated from within, this competitive interaction of opinion-makers is the focal point of the opinion-policy relationship. Out of their interaction, real or imagined, flow the policy alternatives which constitute the dynamics of both the opinion-submitting and the opinion-making processes. Both decision-makers and opinion-holders look to the opinion-making public—the latter for guidance on possible attitudes toward broad issues, and the former for cues as to the particular choices upon which their day-to-day deliberations might be based. In other words, while the mass and attentive publics set the outer and inner limits of the opinion-policy relationship, the opinion-making public determines its structure and content within these limits. If most opinion-makers are not activated by a particular issue, then public discussion of that issue will be narrow and lethargic, leaving decision-makers free to act as they please so long as they can handle the demands of the special-interest opinion-makers who have a stake in the issue and who enjoy unusual prerogatives in the absence of widespread debate. On the other hand, if many types of opinion-makers utilize their access to the opinion-making process, then public discussion of an issue will be extensive and the role of the special-interest opinion-makers will be minimized accordingly. Of course, decision-makers may still be free to act as they please if the extensive discussion between crisscrossing segments of opinion-makers and their followers becomes so competitive as to preclude the emergence of clearcut guide lines to policy. Or, as Almond suggests, extensive competition may lead to unreliability and instability as decision-makers waver back and forth in an effort to cope with conflicting and confusing guide lines.[16]

Chapter 6

CHANNELS OF OPINION

CIRCULATION

Having outlined the various participants in the opinion-making process, let us now look more closely at the channels of communication, both personal and impersonal, by which ideas and information circulate. We need a perspective on how opinions are disseminated throughout the society when, for example, a situation develops abroad which is so novel that no previous opinions about it exist anywhere in the nation. In order to get a meaningful picture of the process that unfolds after opinions have been formed by opinion-makers, we need a close-up—an X-ray as it were—of the circulatory system that carries opinions to the various strata and segments of the public.

As the analysis proceeds we shall outline three primary, seven secondary, and innumerable tertiary channels of communication that convey opinions throughout the circulatory system. The primary channels include the personal, mass, and organizational media. Four types of mass media and three types of organizational media comprise the seven secondary channels, while further breakdowns of each of these and an almost infinite number of face-to-face situations constitute the innumerable tertiary channels through which opinions flow. Our X-ray will further show that all the channels traverse the circulatory system horizontally within the opinion-making public and vertically from it to the other two publics. Only the personal media, however, will be seen to traverse the attentive and mass publics in a horizontal direction.

The Personal Media

As previously indicated, the personal media are those forms of communication used by persons in direct contact with one another, either face-to-face, over the telephone, or by mail. But personal communication involves more than physical, verbal, or written contact. By definition, persons who engage in personal communication must have the opportunity to interact with one another, to exchange opinions freely and continually. The notion of *exchange,* not that of proximity, is conceived to be the distinguishing characteristic of personal communication. Hence a lecture delivered before a large audience is not considered face-to-face communication even though the lecturer is within eye-range of his hearers. As long as the lecture remains structured and opinions cannot be freely exchanged, the situation is regarded as mass or organizational communication. However, if after the lecture some members of the audience gather around the lecturer and argue with him, then the lecture situation is considered to have been replaced by a face-to-face one.

It follows that personal communication can occur without the participants being acquainted with each other.

Ordinarily such communication does take place between acquaintances, but, as in the post-lecture situation, conceivably both opinion-makers and opinion-holders can participate in face-to-face situations without prior acquaintanceship. Members of a panel discussion, to cite another example, are able to exchange opinions and therefore engage in personal communication even though they may not have been previously aware of one another's existence.

The Impersonal Media: Mass versus Organizational Media

If personal communication involves the opportunity to exchange opinions, it follows that impersonal communication implies the absence of this opportunity. Since the impersonal media always involve large numbers of people, why do we bother to distinguish between mass and organizational media? Why not simply designate both types as mass media? The answer stems from a desire to avoid the ambiguities which, as noted in Chapter 1, confound current usage of the concept of mass media. It will be recalled that the mass media are either specifically catalogued as newspapers, magazines, books, television, radio, and motion pictures; or they are more generally defined as those channels which reach large, heterogeneous, and anonymous audiences. Neither of these definitions, however, was found to account satisfactorily for all the forms of communication which are not of a face-to-face kind. Thus it seems prudent to develop a restrictive definition of the mass media and to account for the important impersonal channels that are frequently overlooked by adopting the new concept of organizational media.

Henceforth, then, the term "mass media" refers to those impersonal instruments of communicaton that are intended for, and made available to, *anyone* who is able to utilize them within their distributive limits; whereas "organizational media" refers to those impersonal instruments intended *only* for, and made available *only* to, members or potential members of an organization or association who are able or want to utilize them. The potential audience of an organizational medium, in other words, is differentiated in terms of common affiliation with an organized group, whereas the potential audience of a mass medium is undifferentiated in an affiliational sense.

The Mass Media

It is important to emphasize that only in this one respect are the audiences of the mass media undifferentiated. It is a common fallacy to posit the mass media as being directed at or used by the entire population. This may be the case in small and homogeneous countries like the United Kingdom, but few, if any, media reach the entire American public. Perhaps a few national magazines and the three major broadcasting networks come close to being mass media with completely undifferentiated audiences, although even these offer balanced reading or listening content in order to cater to differentiated tastes among their potential audiences. A preponderance of the mass media, however, is explicitly directed at some differentiated segment of the population. The great majority, as the definition states, have distributive limits, which means that their potential audiences are differentiated in some way, though not as a structured or organized group. These distributive limits may be geographic, economic, ethnic, racial, or cultural. Examples come readily to mind: It is usually necessary to live in California to read California newspapers, reside in or around New York to hear New York radio stations, be able to pay for a television set to become a viewer, speak Italian to read *Il Progresso Italiano,* be a Negro to be interested in reading the magazine *Ebony,* or be a highbrow to want to subscribe to *The New Yorker.*

Of course it is true that Californians, New Yorkers,

Italians, Negroes, and highbrows constitute groups in the sense that each can be described by a common characteristic. They may even be groups in the sense that the common characteristic fosters a feeling of identification and affiliation among those who possess it. Nevertheless, since membership or potential membership in a structured organization or association does not underlie the characteristics or the sense of affiliation which make up these groups, the media which have distributive limits corresponding to these groups are classified as mass rather than organizational media. Nor is this distinction between the two types of impersonal media modified by the fact that both types may be addressed to, and draw upon, very similar audiences. For example, while *Ebony* is classified as a mass medium, a publication of the National Association for the Advancement of Colored People would be considered an organizational medium—even though the readership of both magazines is predominantly Negro.

Depending upon their structure and distributive limits, mass media vary considerably in the manner and speed with which they circulate opinions about foreign policy issues. These variations can be classified in a variety of ways. Account can be taken of structural differences by reference to the printed media and the electronic media, each of which can in turn be subdivided in terms of such conventional categories as newspapers, magazines, and books on the one hand, and radio, television, and motion pictures on the other. The time dimension can be handled by separating, say, daily, weekly, monthly, and quarterly publications. Geographic differentiations can be classified by distinguishing the local media from the cosmopolitan, regional, and national media. Then there are the economic, ethnic, racial, and cultural differentiations cited above, each of which can be further subdivided in an almost unlimited number of ways. Mass media can also be classified according to subject matter, distinguishing, for example, between those that focus on world and public affairs and those oriented to the fields of art or entertainment.

A treatise could be written on the implications for the circulation of foreign-policy opinion of each of the foregoing types of mass media, but here we want only to call attention to these differences by way of avoiding the common and tempting assumption that all mass media make the same or similar contributions to the circulatory system. To emphasize this point, let us look more closely at the distinction between the *printed* media and the *electronic* media. Such a distinction is necessitated, not because it is categorically tidy, but because the structural differences between the printed and electronic media lead to significant behavioral differences. Whereas the electronic media circulate opinions more quickly and over a wider range than the printed media, the latter distribute them in a more thorough and enduring fashion than do the former. Let us consider, for example, the way in which a novel situation would be handled by each type. The electronic media would immediately report the item over the air, thereby bringing news of it into the homes or cars of vast millions of opinion-holders. In addition to a brief outline of the background and portent of the situation, the electronic media might also carry short excerpts from comments which a few opinion-makers (such as the President or a Senator) issued in response to it. The first account of the situation would be periodically supplemented by equally abbreviated accounts of its development in the days, weeks, and months that followed. Thus, within a matter of minutes, great multitudes of opinion-holders are kept informed of the latest upheavals in the crisis. Moreover, the electronic media operate through the auditory sense, which may well be more important to the processes whereby opinions become internalized than is the visual sense through which the printed media operate.

On the other hand, the same structural features which

enable the electronic media to circulate opinions rapidly, widely, and effectively also foster opinions which are necessarily attenuated and transitory. The spoken word takes much longer to communicate than does the written word, so that there is not time enough for extensive and thorough coverage of a situation by electronic media. Even hour-long accounts, attempting to provide background and detail, are inevitably truncated. Thus instead of being presented as a complex issue, with intricate sources and ramifications, the situation is reduced to a problem with one or two major aspects stemming from one or two causes and involving one or two potential consequences. In addition, electronically distributed opinions do not remain very long in the circulatory system. Indeed, their duration is no greater than the speed of sound. Except for tape recordings in the possession of broadcasting companies, electronically circulated opinions cease to exist as soon as they have been transmitted. This means that if an opinion-holder's mind wanders during the broadcast, or if he is confused by the commentary, he cannot rectify his absent-mindedness or his confusion. There is no way of turning back the radio or television dial and listening to the account again from the beginning.

In contrast to the electronic media, the printed media are much more thorough and permanent. Issues and situations can be treated as elaborately as desired. Any situation may become the subject of one or more books devoted to its various causes, aspects, and potential outcomes. Even the columns of a daily newspaper can provide considerably more coverage than can the electronic media on a given issue. Furthermore, and no less important, the absent-minded or confused opinion-holder can always start the newspaper, magazine, or book over again from the beginning; he can mull over what he reads, put it aside, and then return to it days or weeks later. The printed word is, in fact, so permanent that we construct libraries to house it. However, being more thorough in content and more time-consuming in production, the printed media cannot distribute opinions and information instantaneously. There is often a substantial time lag between an event and its description and interpretation by the printed media, especially by weekly, monthly, or quarterly publications. Similarly, while books may be written on any situation, their contents may be outdated by the time they are published. Nor are the printed media structured to reach such vast audiences as the electronic media. No single issue of a newspaper or magazine is read by half as many people as listen to a single radio or television program. Some readers may have a thorough understanding of a situation, but innumerable listeners will at least have heard of it. Finally, it might be hypothesized that the very thoroughness and permanence of the printed media discourage many opinion-holders from paying close attention to foreign-policy issues. It takes time to read; it takes patience to comprehend complexity; it takes interest to enjoy detail—qualities which many opinion-holders do not possess and which many printed media require.

Quality versus Popular Media

These differences between the two basic structural types of mass media lead to the logical probability that, leaving aside the personal and organizational media, opinions circulate more extensively via the electronic than the printed media among apathetic and disinterested members of the mass public, and more extensively via the printed media among active and interested members of the attentive and opinion-making publics. Regardless of whether empirical investigation would substantiate this conclusion, it does suggest that the channels of the circulatory system are differently structured as they pass from one to another of the three strata of the public. One of these variations constitutes a second set of major mass media categories which seems worthy of further elaboration, namely, the distinction between what shall hereinafter be designated *quality* media and *popular* media. Here the difference is not one of structure, but of content. Quality media are those which treat foreign-policy issues seriously, extensively, and continuously; whereas popular media are those which treat these matters in a simplified, abridged, and erratic fashion if they deal with them at all. Those newspapers usually described as "tabloids" are examples of popular media, as are those columnists and commentators who treat a foreign-policy situation in the same vein as they would a sex scandal or a sporting event. Certain national magazines also fall in this category. Among the quality media are newspapers like *The New York Times,* opinion magazines like *Harper's* or *The Reporter,* news magazines like *Time* or *Newsweek,* columnists like Walter Lippmann, commentators like Edward R. Murrow, and television programs like "See It Now."

Obviously, the differences between the quality and popular media are not coextensive with those which distinguish the printed and electronic media. Both types of content flow through each of these two structural forms. But despite this overlapping, the quality-popular distinction is a crucial one. Consider again how each type would handle a novel situation that occurs abroad. The popular media would tend to ignore the situation until a grave crisis developed, at which point they would circulate sensational and oversimplified headlines. On the other hand, the quality media would sustain a continuous flow of considered opinion about the situation from its inception, would debate it in depth, and would place it in proper perspective. In short, the popular media are more suited to the interests of the mass public and the quality media to those of the attentive and opinion-making publics. Indeed, by virtue of their different modes of handling foreign-policy issues, the popular media contribute to *both* the passivity and superficial moods of the mass public, whereas the quality media foster active concern and structured opinion on the part of the other two publics. As one observer puts it, the quality media

> take an active part in the structuring of issues. They participate in foreign policy discussion continually. They reach into the formal governmental agencies and among the nongovernmental opinion leaders. They help create a kind of laboratory atmosphere in which foreign policy ideas can be tested out through the use of responsible speculation and imagination. They constitute a "feedback" on the consequences of policy decisions, and furnish the necessary basis for the constant process of modifying and adapting decisions which have already been made.[1]

The Organizational Media

Having elaborated upon the personal and mass media, let us now take a more extended look at the organizational media, which, it will be recalled, are defined as those impersonal instruments of communication that are intended only for and made available only to members or potential members of an organization or association who are able or want to utilize them.* It should be readily apparent at the outset that the organizational media can be subcategorized in much the same way as the mass media. Since the one variable which distinguishes them from the mass media is not based upon differences in structure or content, it follows that the electronic, printed, quality, and popular classifications can also be applied to types of organizational media. Hence, for example, while a newspaper sold on newsstands is a printed mass medium, a trade-union newspaper made available to union members would be classified

* The communications networks of both nonvoluntary organizations and voluntary associations are subsumed by this definition. For example, both the monthly house organ of a corporation and the weekly newspaper of a labor union are considered organizational media, even though corporations are classified as organizations and unions as associations.

as a printed organizational medium. The distinction between open-and-closed-circuit television programs illustrates how an electronic instrument of communication can
serve as either a mass or an organizational medium. Publications of the Foreign Policy Association, which tend to
be consistently and analytically devoted to foreign affairs,
are good examples of quality organizational media, whereas those of the American Legion, which tend to be more
irregular and emotional in their orientation to foreign-
policy matters, might be categorized as popular organizational media.

The foregoing examples raise the question of how to
classify literature which organizations do not confine to
their memberships and may even prepare especially for
the general public. If such materials are directed at potential members by way of recruiting them into the organization, then they would be considered organizational media.
If, on the other hand, the materials are designed to arouse
wide public support of particular policies in which the
organization is interested, then they would be classified as
mass media. In other words, organizational media do not
necessarily convey all the opinions which emanate from
organizations or associations. Rather, they are conceived
as conveying only those opinions which circulate among
parts or all of the organization's membership. Many associations, especially civic-interest types, frequently use mass
media in order to serve those organizational purposes
which involve informing and activating a much wider public than the one circumscribed by their membership. Indeed, the widespread development and institutionalization
of the position of director of public relations indicates the
large extent to which organizations and associations find it
necessary to utilize the mass media for their own purposes.
(Interestingly, a major type of organizational medium is
the converse of this process: not infrequently association
leaders attempt to maintain the commitment of their members by distributing to them press releases or reprints of

materials which they previously distributed through the mass media to a wider public.)

Moreover, opinions may circulate via both organizational and mass media at the same time. For example, a lecture which an association presents for its members might also be carried over a radio network and covered by the press, or the association's public relations specialist might see to it that an account of the event was distributed to and by the mass media. Conceivably, in fact, communication can occur simultaneously via all three types of media: personal, organizational, and mass. A panel discussion sponsored by an organization for its members and carried over the radio would be an instance of such three-way circulation: opinions exchanged among members of the panel would not only circulate through personal channels, but would also reach members of the immediate audience through organizational channels and the undifferentiated radio audience through mass channels. Presidential nominating conventions are another example of multiple circulation; here opinions move through many secondary and tertiary channels of communication, as well as through the three primary types.

In addition to subcategorizing the organizational media along lines similar to those established for the mass media, account must be taken of those opinion-circulating methods which are uniquely a function of organizational or associational activity. Since these methods are not usually viewed from the larger perspective of the circulatory system, the language of communications research does not provide labels for the three main subcategories of organizational media which need to be discussed. Hence, for two of these it has been necessary to make up words, and the reader is asked to suffer distortion of the English language on the grounds that these terms are more suggestive of the phenomena they describe than any others that might have been used.

Assemblematic Media. The category of assemblematic media includes all the various ways in which members of an association are assembled together for the purpose of, among other things, systematically communicating opinions about some subject. Panel discussions, lectures, and conferences are typical examples of this type of communication. The importance of these assemblematic media is emphasized by the fact that often they serve as a basis for situations of multiple circulation. As noted above, simultaneous communication through personal and mass media ordinarily takes place at an associational gathering. Obviously this antecedent character of the assemblematic media gives associational opinion-makers a unique kind of access to the mass channels of the circulatory system.

Not all associational gatherings are subsumed by this category, for the definition applies only to those gatherings that foster communication in some *systematic* or structured way. Thus gatherings convened for purely social purposes, such as dances or picnics, do not come within the scope of the category, albeit the fox trot and the box lunch provide ample opportunity for face-to-face communication.

In a sense, of course, the assemblematic media are also settings for, rather than means of, communication. Assembling a membership in one place is not the same as exposing it to ideas from a rostrum. Strictly speaking, the lecture hall and the conference room are organizational settings within which media of communication are employed. However, we have avoided this distinction on the ground that opinion-makers would not subscribe to it. Rather, it seems likely that they view assemblages as they do any other *means* of circulating ideas. One can readily imagine associational opinion-makers saying, "This project calls for efforts to place an article in the *Reader's Digest,* but for that one we need to hold a panel discussion."

Perhaps the most significant assemblematic medium is the general membership meeting or convention which most, if not all, associations hold annually or at some regular interval. To be sure, the main business of such meetings, especially those held by special-interest groups, may be far removed from issues of foreign policy. Officers have to be elected; research developments have to be reported; friendships have to be renewed; leading members have to be honored; future plans have to be made or approved. Indeed, these activities are the *raison d'être* of annual conventions, and often their focus does not extend beyond these limited matters which sustain organizational life. When druggists convene, for example, communication centers primarily upon pharmaceutical affairs and not upon foreign affairs, just as professors concentrate upon academic policy rather than foreign policy when they gather at meetings of the American Association of University Professors. Nevertheless, there are several reasons why the annual convention must be considered an important channel in the circulatory system. In the first place, the consequences of foreign policy are so pervasive in modern life that probably most annual meetings touch at least upon some aspect of the prevailing world scene. While such matters may not be the main business of the convention, they are likely to be of peripheral concern. Foreign-policy developments may come up even at a druggists' convention, as when pharmaceutical interests are affected by a lowering of the tariff on foreign cosmetics. Moreover, there are many associations which, for reasons of either civic or special interest, explicitly dwell upon aspects of foreign policy during their annual conventions. Anyone familiar with the contents of the innumerable resolutions which Congressmen daily insert into the *Congressional Record* on behalf of many diverse organizations will recognize that annual conventions do indeed operate as media for circulating opinions about foreign affairs.

There is a second reason why the annual conventions are an important channel in the circulatory system: namely, it is largely under such circumstances that the phenomenon of attention groups comes into being. It will be recalled that attention groups are unorganized and passive segments of the mass public which suddenly and impulsively enter the opinion-making process in the form of structured groups whenever their interests are affected by some aspect of foreign policy. Yet attention groups do not necessarily come into existence because their members, either independently or in response to the urgings of associational opinion-makers, have been simultaneously moved by an issue to become amateur opinion-submitters. Only under rare and extraordinary circumstances do spontaneous and unrelated individual actions occur in such way as to signal the formation of attention groups. Rather, the appearance of joint and united conviction usually develops through speeches or resolutions approved at the formal gatherings of associations. Thus it is through assemblematic media that attention groups often acquire the structure and the recognition which results in an impact upon the opinion-making process. In the aforementioned example of the druggists, this may be the only method by which they can effectively emerge from passivity to protest a change in the import duty on cosmetics.

Another important aspect of the annual convention is the opportunity for expression which it affords certain top opinion-makers outside of the convening association. Whatever else may be scheduled, conventions usually include at least one or two addresses by distinguished persons who have been invited to give their views on some topic pertinent to the goals or activities of the sponsoring association. For obvious reasons, these invitations are often issued to top governmental opinion-makers. Hardly a week passes in which some Cabinet member or legislative leader is not called upon to make a significant address before the annual convention of some organization. The convention platform is thus a major rostrum from which the governmental decision-maker may assume the role of opinion-maker. He can use this assemblematic medium either as a technique for reaching certain segments of the public directly or as a way of having his opinions indirectly introduced into the mass media through press and radio coverage of the convention. Indeed, annual conventions and commencement exercises are perhaps the only occasions consistently available to decision-makers in the executive branch for discursive and uninterrupted expression of opinion in public. At press conferences and legislative hearings, the initiative lies with the questioners, with the result that it is difficult for the speaker to develop a central idea logically and fully. From the associational rostrum, on the other hand, he can deliver an unbroken train of thought that has been previously prepared, pondered over, revised, and committed to paper. In this sense, it is hardly farfetched to observe that access to the floor of the annual convention is to the executive opinion-maker what access to the floor of Congress is to the legislative opinion-maker.

The potential behavior of those in attendance at the annual convention is still another reason for considering it an important channel in the circulatory system. That is, those who attend may subsequently circulate opinions about the foreign-policy issues to which they were introduced at the convention. To be sure, the conventioners will, depending upon the association, be located at various points in the opinion-making process. Certain types of meetings, such as the annual conference of the state governors or presidents of land grant colleges, are comprised, by definition, almost exclusively of opinion-makers. Others, such as the annual meetings of the American Economic Association, are probably attended by both opinion-makers and members of the attentive public. Still others, such as the annual convention of the AFL-CIO or of the American Legion, are doubtless composed of members of the opinion-making, attentive, and mass publics. Finally, in all probability some conventions, especially those of special-interest associations, such as the druggists, are made up primarily of members of the mass public.

Regardless of the strata to which they belong, however,

conventioners may find that the opinions to which they are exposed at these meetings are just as adoptable as those which they might acquire through other media. For opinion-makers in attendance, the convention serves as a basis for engaging in the opinion-forming process. Interaction with colleagues, for example, may help individual state governors or college presidents to hammer out opinions which they might otherwise not have arrived at so precisely and promptly. For members of the attentive and mass publics in attendance, opinions heard at the convention may be especially easy to internalize. These opinions, after all, are contacted in the context of associational camaraderie and commitment, factors which undoubtedly heighten receptivity to ideas. In addition, many conventioners from the attentive and mass publics may subsequently be able to assume the role of opinion leader (as distinguished from opinion-maker), either because attendance at such an occasion is itself a status-conferring experience or because it reflects prior status in a community, profession, or occupation. Thus it is quite possible that the opinions expressed at a convention will reach many people who neither attended the proceedings nor heard about them through the mass media.

The previous paragraph contains an important modification of the "two-step flow" process of communication. It suggests that the first step in the process, that of supplying opinion leaders with the opinions which they disseminate in face-to-face situations, can be performed by the assemblematic media as well as by the mass media. Indeed, these and other organizational media may even be the favorite source of opinions for the many opinion leaders who maintain active membership in voluntary associations. More prestige attaches to attending a convention than to reading a newspaper, so that the typical opinion leader may be inclined to cite viewpoints acquired through assemblematic media more readily than those picked up in the mass media. Such remarks as "I heard the Secretary of

State at our convention in St. Louis insist that . . ." or, "At the lecture sponsored by our organization last week I heard the President of General Motors say that . . ." make an excellent preface to the expression of one's own opinions. Thus the assemblematic media may supply the opinion leader, not only with ideas and information, but also with a capacity to legitimate his opinions in an impressive way.[2]

Memorandummatic Media. Closely related to the assemblematic media is a second subcategory of organizational media which, for want of a better term, will be referred to as the "memorandummatic" media. This classification includes all the various forms in which associations circulate written memoranda relative to their activities and goals among all or most of their members. Excluded from this definition, however, are memoranda which are not intended for the entire membership of an organization or even for major segments thereof, such as communications to the administrative staff. Rather, the definition subsumes such media as newsletters, pamphlets, house organs, and fact sheets, all of which are circulated widely within an organization. Since associations do not convene very often as a body, the memorandummatic media are the main instrument for maintaining organizational life during the intervals between conventions. Via these media, members receive a constant stream of notices, information, opinions, and recommendations from associational headquarters. To be sure, foreign affairs are not necessarily a major focus of the memoranda. As in the case of the annual convention, the contents of such media will, depending on the association, vary greatly with respect to the attention paid to world affairs. Usually, however, the written and unwritten rules governing their contents are sufficiently flexible to permit the inclusion of relevant items pertaining to issues of foreign policy. A column of comment is a standard feature of memorandummatic media and this provides associational opinion-makers with an opportunity to refer to foreign affairs if they so desire.

Perhaps the most important memorandummatic medium is the bulletin which virtually all organizations publish at regular intervals and which is usually considered to be the official publication of the association issuing it. The bulletin may be a brief newsletter or a lengthy journal. It may be issued weekly, monthly, or quarterly. It may be disseminated free or, as is more frequently the case, it may be a service rendered members in exchange for membership dues. Regardless of its form and manner of distribution, the associational bulletin is a major (and perhaps the only) link between the geographically dispersed and otherwise heterogeneous membership of an association. Unlike the annual convention, which is not attended by the entire membership, the bulletin is received by all of the association's members. Furthermore, it has a number of features which give to the association a sense of continuity and unity that other organizational media cannot and do not provide: (1) the bulletin arrives at specified and regular intervals; (2) issues are consecutively numbered; (3) it contains news about the association, its officers, activities, and aspirations; and (4) it can be kept as a record of associational development and precedent. (The extent to which the bulletin's mailing list is sought and used by outsiders who have a particular message to bring to association members enlarges even further its contribution to the circulatory system. Anyone who receives substantial amounts of nonpersonal mail will recognize that the mailing lists of associational bulletins constitute a complex communications network which extends throughout the society.)

The bulletins of associations comprised mainly of opinion-makers would seem to be particularly important channels of the circulatory system. For it is in such media that opinion-makers are reminded of their role as opinion-makers. The journals of professional societies, for example, periodically devote space to analyses of the leadership responsibilities of their members, to the place of their profession in society, and to the larger obligations which their positions entail. Indeed, occasionally they may even circulate opinions about foreign policy which are posited as appropriate to members of the profession receiving the journal.[3] Not only do these media remind opinion-makers of their access to the opinion-making process, but they also provide a forum for the discussion of international affairs. For instance, the relevance of nuclear weapons to foreign policy has been the subject of numerous articles in a variety of bulletins, each successive analysis noting where it differs from its predecessors. This type of continuous debate suggests that such media can be as important as a setting for the interaction through which opinion-makers formulate their attitudes toward foreign-policy issues as is a face-to-face situation.

Presumably the bulletins which circulate among members of the mass and attentive publics also contribute substantially to the opinion-making process. Since the opinions expressed are likely to be more in harmony with the interests of the association's readers than those circulated by the mass media, the bulletins and other memorandummatic media enable association members in the mass and attentive publics to internalize opinions that mirror the societal vantage points in which they are located. Moreover, by alerting readers to those points at which foreign policy impinges upon associational interests, such media may lay the groundwork for the formation of attention groups at annual conventions. For the same reasons, memorandummatic media may also supplement the convention as a source of opinions for opinion leaders among their readership.

Programmatic Media. A third subcategory of organizational media subsumes what can be called the "programmatic" media. These are defined as the various means by which the future circulation of opinions is either facilitated, ensured, or programed. Examples of programmatic media are arranging an agenda, compiling a speakers' list, developing topics or materials for discussion, and distributing plans for mobilizing community interest in an issue. The efforts of more than a few associations in the world affairs field are almost exclusively based on use of programmatic media. The Association of International Relations Clubs, for instance, is mainly concerned with fostering and channeling activity on the part of its affiliated organizations. In other words, programmatic media do not in themselves circulate opinions about foreign policy; rather, they permit or assist the subsequent circulation of such opinions. Thus, planning the agenda for a conference would constitute use of the programmatic medium, whereas the conference itself would be classified as an assemblematic medium. Similarly, the distribution of a memorandum containing a list of speakers available to groups would be considered programmatic, but a memorandum containing reprints of their speeches would be considered memorandummatic.

Admittedly this category includes activities which, strictly speaking, may not be means of communication. However, such activities are so intrinsic to the circulatory system that it seems appropriate to analyze them separately. In particular, if we did not take the programmatic media into account, we would be overlooking a major aspect of the role of associational opinion-makers, many of whom do not themselves circulate opinions as much as they initiate indirect circulation by getting others to formulate opinions about issues which they have selected. By arranging a conference agenda or a discussion group, the associational opinion-maker determines the context within which activity will occur and the issues around which it will revolve. Hence the opinions which subsequently circulate are due as much to his use of a programmatic medium as to whatever may take place at the conference or in the discussion group. While he may not initiate the circulation of a specific opinion through the programmatic media, his efforts are consequential in the sense that he establishes the width, depth, and direction of the channel through which opinions will flow. Surely, this is what happens when opinion-makers affiliated with the Foreign Policy Association annually distribute kits enabling its members to hold discussions on "great decisions" facing the world's leaders. To be sure, the kits include "individual opinion ballots" designed to encourage independent judgment on the part of the discussants. Nevertheless, it is expected that members will use their judgment and cast their ballots *after* participating in a discussion for which the Association has previously supplied all the equipment, both intellectual and mechanical. The 1959 kit, for instance, is described by an Association brochure as follows:

> Great Decisions . . . 1959—Set of nine fact sheets (including introductory sheet) designed for group discussion (with or without trained discussion leaders) and for classroom use at secondary or college level. Particularly suitable for 8- or 9-week discussion program or teaching unit. Translates into terms understandable to the layman the current national debate on broad-scale review of U.S. foreign policy. Examines technological, economic and political revolutions of our times and defines the policy issues which call for citizen understanding and decision. Poster-size sheets, printed both sides, with nonpartisan factual data, maps, charts, bibliographies and discussion questions. Individual opinion ballots included with eight of the fact sheets. The set: $1.00.

Interestingly, it seems likely that some associational opinion-makers, especially those that view discussion and activity on the part of their membership as a good in itself, fail to recognize the indirect effects which stem from use of the programmatic media. In spite of claims that they are interested only in having opinions circulate, and not in the opinions themselves, they do not hesitate to disseminate materials which specify the problems to be discussed and the main lines which discussion should follow.[4]

With respect to the relative effectiveness of the organizational media, it seems reasonable to conclude that they do not circulate opinions as swiftly or as widely as do the mass media. Whereas opinions are carried quickly by newspapers or over television, it takes time before members of an organization can be reached, either individually or collectively. On the other hand, conceivably opinions circulated via organizational media are more enduring than those distributed by the mass media because the former are capable of holding their audience longer. Associational opinion-makers can keep an issue alive by elaborating upon its major features, following it up, servicing it periodically with revised memoranda or a new lecture series, and so on; whereas the mass media have an undifferentiated audience and are thus less able to concentrate continually on any single issue.

Of course, any comparison between organizational and mass media must necessarily be speculative. Empirical data pertaining to their operation and consequences have not yet been developed, and it may be that we have exaggerated their importance in the circulatory system. The foregoing discussion indicates, however, that it would be unwise, in the absence of contrary evidence, not to assume that the organizational media constitute important channels of communication which are neither duplicated by nor subsumed by the mass or personal media.

Chapter 7

TOWARD A THEORY OF
THE OPINION-POLICY
RELATIONSHIP

Having made his way thus far, the reader may wonder exactly what would be accomplished if data were to be coded and examined in terms of the many categories and subcategories that have been set forth. Would empirical application of this scheme, he might properly ask, add materially to our understanding of the opinion-policy relationship? Granted that a more coherent and accurate description may result from the use of precise and operational concepts, do these permit more accurate predictions about the conditions under which public opinion will have varying effects upon the deliberations of foreign-policy officials? Can theoretical propositions be logically derived from this breakdown of the relationship into three social processes, three strata of the public, sixteen kinds of opin-

ion-makers, and three primary and seven secondary channels of communication?

Strictly speaking, the answer to these questions is "No."
The foregoing analysis does not contain the linkages between the various publics, opinion-makers, and communications media. It notes how and where the decision-making,
opinion-submitting, and opinion-making processes overlap,
but it does not include any estimates of when and why
these interrelations occur in one form rather than another.
Indeed, it will be recalled that the concept of influence
was purposely avoided, that a choice was made to analyze
the different publics, opinion-makers, and media in action
terms rather than in terms of their motivation or effectiveness. From the outset, in other words, it was recognized
that no matter how elaborate and operational our conceptual framework turned out to be, it would not in itself
reveal the causal factors through which the opinion-policy
relationship is consummated.

In a more general sense, however, an affirmative response may be given to the queries raised above. By con-
structing an elaborate and operational framework, we have
presumably located the key points at which influence is
operative. Hence, if empirical data classified along these
lines were to result in extensive knowledge of each com-
ponent of the opinion-making process, we should be in
a position to derive reliable inferences about the flow of
influence. In turn, these inferences should enable us to
formulate more accurate predictions about the opinion-
policy relationship than is presently possible. Indeed, if
this scheme or one like it were applied to various kinds of
foreign-policy issues, there is no reason why an integrated,
comprehensive, and useful set of theoretical propositions
could not be developed. In this general sense, then, it
seems reasonable to assert that a great deal might be accomplished if data were coded and examined in terms of
our framework. The ingredients of a theory are there, and

empirical investigation should facilitate linking them up into a theoretical whole.

What might such a theory of the opinion-policy relationship look like? In all probability, it would be composed of four interrelated parts. One would encompass propositions about the varying degrees of activity that different types of foreign-policy issues are likely to precipitate among various segments of the opinion-making public. Another part would consist of propositions about the varying states of the circulatory system that are likely to be produced by different amounts and kinds of activity on the part of different groups of opinion-makers. A third set of propositions would deal with the varying kinds and amounts of opinion-submitting that are likely to stem from different states of the circulatory system. The fourth part of the theory would embrace propositions pertaining to the various ways in which the decision-making process is likely to be affected by differing forms of the opinion-making and opinion-submitting processes.

The potentiality of theoretical development along these lines becomes immediately apparent when one speculates about the ways in which two different types of issues might differentially activate the opinion-policy relationship. For example, a comparison of how the relationship might be affected by a diplomatic issue (say, the negotiation and ratification of a treaty) and an economic issue (say, the formulation and adoption of a foreign-aid program) brings to mind a number of hypotheses. In the first place, it seems likely that the aid issue would precipitate more intense activity on the part of more segments of the opinion-making public than would the treaty issue. Ordinarily treaties deal with seemingly remote and legal problems, whereas foreign aid is closely linked to such close-to-home matters as taxes and employment. Thus the treaty issue would probably arouse activity on the part of a broad cross section of civic-interest opinion-makers, but of only a few special-interest opinion-makers. The ranks of the latter, however, would probably be greatly swelled by the foreign-aid issue. In view of the bread-and-butter nature of foreign aid, it could also be reasoned that since all members of Congress must ultimately participate in appropriating funds for the program, and inasmuch as this responsibility puts them in the position of having to be pampered and importuned, the issue would tend to isolate legislative opinion-makers, both behaviorally and attitudinally, from other segments of the national opinion-making public.

Similar reasoning leads to these additional hypotheses:

1. That the economic issue would foster greater opinion-making activity on the part of legislators than would its diplomatic counterpart.

2. That activity on the part of local opinion-makers would be at a maximum on the foreign-aid issue and at a minimum on the treaty issue.

3. That discussion of the treaty would be confined primarily to quality media, whereas both quality and mass media would circulate opinions about foreign aid.

4. That only a trickle of opinion about the treaty would flow through organizational channels, whereas a torrent of ideas about foreign aid would be introduced into them.

5. That the attentive and mass publics would be more familiar with the foreign-aid than with the treaty issue.

6. That on the foreign-aid issue, the opinion-submitting process would be more directed toward legislative than executive opinion-makers, whereas the opposite pattern would prevail with respect to the treaty issue.

7. That proposed and ratified forms of the treaty would resemble each other more closely than would the proposed and adopted foreign-aid measures.

Of course, these hypotheses might prove to be erroneous when subjected to empirical verification.[1] Or they might require revision when enlarged to account for still other types of issues. For example, it is provocative to speculate about the form which the opinion-policy relationship would take with respect to a war-peace issue (say, a Soviet threat to Berlin), or an uprising abroad (say, in Hungary), or a major technological development (say, in outer space). However, even in their present form, and irrespective of their validity, the foregoing hypotheses do indicate the possibilities of developing a theory of the opinion-policy relationship from the framework here presented. For if a series of propositions of this sort can be tested and validated, and if in so doing the key variables can be manipulated through the kinds of historical situations chosen for examination, then eventually it should be possible to predict the nature of the governmental response to various types of issues whenever they arise.

Notes and References

Chapter 1. THE STATE OF THE FIELD: A CRITIQUE

1. For a persuasive analysis of the scantiness of our knowledge in this area, see Bernard C. Cohen, *The Influence of Non-Governmental Groups on Foreign Policy-Making* (Boston: World Peace Foundation, 1959), pp. 1-6. The same author, in *The Political Process and Foreign Policy: The Making of the Japanese Peace Settlement* (Princeton: Princeton University Press, 1957), has himself provided some of the few available data that are relevant to the processes through which the opinion-policy relationship is consummated.

2. The potential usefulness of organizing research around the growth and dissolution of issues is emphasized and analyzed by W. Phillips Davison, "The Public Opinion Process," *Public Opinion Quarterly*, Vol. 22, Summer 1958, pp. 91-106.

3. Gabriel A. Almond, *The American People and Foreign Policy* (New York: Harcourt, Brace & Co., 1950).

4. See Elihu Katz and Paul F. Lazarsfeld, *Personal Influence* (Glencoe: Free Press, 1955), *passim,* and

Elihu Katz, "The Two-Step Flow of Communication: An Up-to-date Report on an Hypothesis," *Public Opinion Quarterly,* Vol. 21, Spring 1957, pp. 61-78.

5. Gabriel A. Almond, "Public Opinion and National Security Policy," *Public Opinion Quarterly,* Vol. 20, Summer 1956, p. 376.

6. For elaborations of this definition, see Charles R. Wright, *Mass Communication* (New York: Random House, 1959), pp. 13-14; Eliot Friedson, "Communications Research and the Concept of the Mass," in Wilbur Schramm (ed.), *The Process and Effects of Mass Communication* (Urbana: University of Illinois Press, 1954), p. 381.

7. Gabriel A. Almond and Elmo Roper are two observers who have suggested other categories at the mass and face-to-face level, the former in "Public Opinion and National Security," *op. cit.,* p. 374, and the latter in "Who Tells the Story-tellers," *Saturday Review,* July 31, 1954, p. 32. Concerned about the special characteristics of those media that reach elite groups or persons who share a serious interest in public affairs, both men draw a distinction between a daily tabloid and a newspaper like *The New York Times.* They would both classify the former as a mass medium, but would call attention to the homogeneity of the *Times's* audience by calling it either a "quality" (Almond) or a "class" (Roper) medium. However, important and useful as additional categories of this sort obviously are, they still do not account for all the possible means of communication which are neither of a mass nor a face-to-face kind. There are other kinds of homogeneity besides shared interest in public affairs. Conferences and history lectures, for example, cannot be easily classified in any of these major categories. Similarly, it seems inappropriate to regard professional

journals and technical books as quality or class media even though they are distributed to audiences which are homogeneous in at least one respect.

8. Almond, *The American People and Foreign Policy,* p. 138; C. Wright Mills, *The Power Elite* (New York: Oxford University Press, 1956), *passim;* Harold D. Lasswell, Daniel Lerner, and C. Easton Rothwell, *The Comparative Study of Elites* (Stanford: Stanford University Press, 1952), Ch. 2.

9. Richard C. Snyder and Edgar S. Furniss, Jr., *American Foreign Policy* (New York: Rinehart & Co., 1954), p. 525.

10. Kenneth P. Adler and David Bobrow, "Interest and Influence in Foreign Affairs," *Public Opinion Quarterly,* Vol. 20, Spring 1956, pp. 89-101.

11. Elmo Roper, *op. cit.,* p. 26.

12. David Riesman, "Private People and Public Policy," *Bulletin of the Atomic Scientists,* Vol. 15, May 1959, p. 204.

13. Alfred O. Hero, *Opinion Leaders in American Communities* (Boston: World Peace Foundation, 1959), *passim.*

14. Charles O. Lerche, Jr., *Foreign Policy of the American People* (Englewood Cliffs: Prentice-Hall, 1958), pp. 71-72.

15. Robert K. Merton, *Social Theory and Social Structure* (revised ed., Glencoe: Free Press, 1957), pp. 393 ff.

16. Almond, *The American People and Foreign Policy,* p. 138.

17. Snyder and Furniss, *op. cit.,* p. 138.

18. Lerche, *op. cit.,* p. 71.

19. The need for a re-examination of key concepts has also been demonstrated by Harvey Glickman, whose impressive critique of the confusion and ambiguity that usually characterizes the term "public opinion" contains the seeds of a conceptualization not unlike the one developed here. See his article, "Viewing Public Opinion in Politics: A Common Sense Approach," *Public Opinion Quarterly*, Vol. 23, Winter 1959-1960, pp. 495-504.

Chapter 2. THE FLOW OF INFLUENCE VERSUS THE FLOW OF OPINION

1. Katz and Lazarsfeld, *op. cit.*, p. 137.

2. For an elaboration of the notion that influence is equivalent to this particular form of causality, see James G. March, "An Introduction to the Theory and Measurement of Influence," *American Political Science Review*, Vol. 49, June 1955, p. 437.

3. See, for example, Dorwin Cartwright and Alvin Zander (eds.), *Group Dynamics* (Evanston: Row, Peterson and Co., 1953), Part Three.

4. For an illustration of how operational definitions of influence narrow the scope of inquiry, see Dahl's brilliant analysis of the ruling elite hypothesis and the limited circumstances under which it can be subjected to empirical verification. Robert A. Dahl, "A Critique of the Ruling Elite Model," *American Political Science Review*, Vol. 52, June 1958, pp. 463-69.

5. Karl W. Deutsch and Lewis J. Edinger, *Germany Rejoins the Powers: Mass Opinion, Interest Groups, and Elites in Contemporary German Foreign Policy* (Stanford: Stanford University Press, 1959), p. 195.

Chapter 4. THE STRATIFICATION OF THE PUBLIC

1. See Katz and Lazarsfeld, *op. cit.,* Chap. 2.

2. For a more elaborate analysis of this conception of the varying composition of the "public," see Glickman, *op. cit.,* pp. 498-501.

3. This pyramidal conception, as well as the analysis of the mass and attentive publics which follows, has been derived from Gabriel Almond's formulation of the opinion-policy relationship (in particular see his *The American People and Foreign Policy,* pp. 138-39). The only major innovation is the labeling of the opinion-making public, which Almond regards as the elite groups. The reasons for this terminological alteration are noted in Chapter 5.

4. See Alfred O. Hero, *Americans in World Affairs* (Boston: World Peace Foundation, 1959), p. 10.

5. The concept of mood and the poles within which it fluctuates are outlined in Almond, *The American People and Foreign Policy,* pp. 53 ff.

6. Almond, "Public Opinion and National Security Policy," p. 376.

7. *Ibid.,* p. 376. Attention groups must not be confused with the attentive public. The distinction between the two is clarified below.

8. *Ibid.,* pp. 376-77.

9. "Foreword," in Katz and Lazarsfeld, *op. cit.,* p. xviii.

10. Almond, "Public Opinion and National Security Policy," p. 377.

Chapter 5. THE OPINION-MAKERS

1. Lasswell, Lerner, and Rothwell, *op. cit.,* p. 6.

2. Snyder and Furniss, *op. cit.,* p. 525 (italics added).

3. Almond, *The American People and Foreign Policy,* p. 138.

4. *Ibid.,* p. 137.

5. Elmo Roper's distinction between the "Great" and the "Lesser Disseminators" also reflects an attempt to account for this national-local dimension of opinion making. ("Foreword," in Katz and Lazarsfeld, *op. cit.,* p. xvii).

6. For some provocative comments about the important role which single-issue opinion-makers may play in the opinion-policy relationship, see Roger Hilsman, "The Foreign-Policy Consensus: An Interim Research Report," *The Journal of Conflict Resolution,* Vol. III, December 1959, pp. 372-73.

7. See Paul F. Lazarsfeld and Robert K. Merton, "Mass Communication, Popular Taste and Organized Social Action," in Lyman Bryson (ed.), *The Communication of Ideas* (New York: Harper & Bros., 1948), p. 101.

8. Cf. Edward Gross, "The Occupation Variable as a Research Category," *American Sociological Review,* Vol. 24, October 1959, pp. 640-49.

9. Somehow, despite terminological and conceptual differences, four basic categories always seem to result from efforts to subdivide the opinion-making public along occupational lines. Snyder and Furniss, for example, consider that "the effective public must be thought of as having four components: a. Organized groups . . . b. Mass communication leaders and mediums . . . c. Teachers, d. Community leaders. . . ."

(*op. cit.,* p. 526). Similarly, Almond classifies "the elite groups which share in the process of policy initiation and formation . . . under four main headings. 1. The political elites . . . 2. The administrative or bureaucratic elites . . . 3. The interest elites . . . 4. . . . the communications elites. . . ." (*The American People and Foreign Policy,* pp. 139-140).

10. A useful and operational definition of this type of group is provided by Maccoby: "The distinguishing characteristics of the voluntary association are that it be private, non-profit, voluntary in that entrance rests on mutual consent while exit is at the will of either party, and formal in that there are offices to be filled in accordance with stipulated rules. These traits serve to differentiate the voluntary association from public and governmental bodies; profit-making corporations and partnerships; family, clan, church, nation and other groups, cliques, or gangs." (Herbert Maccoby, "The Differential Political Activity of Participants in a Voluntary Association," *American Sociological Review,* Vol. 23, October 1958, p. 524.)

11. For an analysis of the difficulties of classifying voluntary associations, see David B. Truman, *The Governmental Process* (New York: Alfred A. Knopf, 1951), pp. 63-65; C. Wayne Gordon and Nicholas Babchuk, "A Typology of Voluntary Associations," *American Sociological Review,* Vol. 24, February 1959, pp. 22-29.

12. The first three of these types are equivalent to the persons covered by Almond's aforementioned communications elite category. The decision to achieve conceptual thoroughness by broadening this category to include all types of institutional opinion-makers, especially businessmen and lawyers, was reinforced by the findings of Adler and Bobrow. These researchers,

in an effort to identify and examine the opinion-makers ("foreign-policy influentials") of a "well-to-do suburb of a large Midwestern city," found that the ranks of opinion-makers "include a substantial number of lawyers and corporation executives, constituting a legal and economic elite which Almond's structural framework does not fully accommodate." (*Op. cit.,* p. 97.)

13. New York: Harper & Bros. (for the Council on Foreign Relations), 1957.

14. Elmo Roper hypothesizes the existence of between 250 and 1,000 "Great Disseminators" and between 15,000 and 50,000 "Lesser Disseminators" ("Foreword," in Katz and Lazarsfeld, *op. cit.,* p. xvii).

15. *The American People and Foreign Policy,* p. 144.

16. *Ibid.,* p. 145.

Chapter 6. CHANNELS OF OPINION CIRCULATION

1. Almond, "Public Opinion and National Security Policy," p. 374.

2. It should be noted that empirical findings descriptive of the effects of the organizational media are virtually nonexistent and that therefore this discussion of the role they play in the circulatory system is based primarily on speculation. For a summary of the few available data that do pertain to the organizational media, see Alfred O. Hero, *Voluntary Organizations in World Affairs Communication* (Boston: World Peace Foundation, 1960), pp. 23-25.

3. See, for example, Neal D. Houghton, "The Challenge to Political Scientists in Recent American Foreign Policy: Scholarship or Indoctrination?" *American Political Science Review,* Vol. 52 (September 1958), pp. 678-88.

4. For evidence that some associational opinion-makers in the world affairs field tend to reason along these lines, see Bernard C. Cohen, *Citizen Education in World Affairs* (Princeton: Center of International Studies, 1953), pp. 63-67.

Chapter 7. TOWARD A THEORY OF THE OPINION-POLICY RELATIONSHIP

1. On the basis of specific cases, however, there is some reason to believe that the hypotheses are well founded. Compare the findings of Bernard C. Cohen's inquiry into the 1951 Japanese peace treaty (*The Political Process and Foreign Policy: The Making of the Japanese Peace Settlement*) with those of H. Field Haviland, Jr., who subjected one year of the policy-making process in the foreign aid field to close examination ("Foreign Aid and the Policy Process: 1957," *American Political Science Review*, Vol. LII, September 1958, pp. 689-724).

Selected Readings

The Opinion-Policy Relationship

There are a few general works on this relationship which can be fruitfully consulted by those who wish to read further about it. Certainly, as indicated, a primary source is Gabriel A. Almond, *The American People and Foreign Policy* (New York: Harcourt, Brace & Co., 1950). A good symposium on various aspects of the relationship is provided by Lester Markel (ed.), *Public Opinion and Foreign Policy* (New York: Harper & Bros., 1949), whereas an excellent case study of the relationship in a particular situation is available in Bernard C. Cohen, *The Political Process and Foreign Policy: The Making of the Japanese Peace Settlement* (Princeton: Princeton University Press, 1957). Raymond H. Dawson, *The Decision to Aid Russia, 1941: Foreign Policy and Domestic Politics* (Chapel Hill: University of North Carolina Press, 1959), is still another good case history of the relationship. A creative case study of how the relationship operates in a foreign country is Karl W. Deutsch and Lewis J. Edinger, *Germany Rejoins the Powers: Mass Opinion, Interest Groups, and Elites in Contemporary German Foreign Policy* (Stanford: Stanford University Press, 1959). At the more philosophical level several books are worthy of a careful reading. Still enormously provocative are John Dewey, *The Public and Its Problems* (New York: Henry Holt & Co., 1927), and Walter Lippmann, *Public Opinion* (New York: The Macmillan Co., 1922). Somewhat more pessimistic treatments of the subject are to be found in Max Beloff, *Foreign Policy and the Democratic Process* (Baltimore: Johns Hopkins Press, 1955) and Walter Lippmann, *Essays in the Public Philosophy* (Boston: Little, Brown & Co., 1955).

Among the many works on the opinion-submitting process in the United States, the following deal primarily with the submission of opinions on foreign-policy issues:

Donald C. Blaisdell, "Pressure Groups, Foreign Policies, and International Politics," *Annals,* Vol. 319 (September 1958), pp. 149-57.

Bernard C. Cohen, *The Influence of Non-Governmental Groups on Foreign Policy-Making* (Boston: World Peace Foundation, 1959).

J. C. Donovan, "The Political Party and Foreign Policy-Making," *World Affairs Quarterly,* April 1957.

Lucian W. Pye, "Effects of Legislative and Administrative Accessibility on Interest Group Politics," *PROD,* Vol. I (January 1958), pp. 11-13.

Leila Sussmann, "Mass Political Letter Writing in America," *Public Opinion Quarterly,* Vol. XXIII (Summer 1959), pp. 203-12.

As for the perceptual circumvention of the opinion-submitting process by policy-makers, see Bernard C. Cohen,

"Foreign Policy Makers and the Press," in James N. Rosenau (ed.), *International Politics and Foreign Policy: A Reader in Theory and Research* (New York: Free Press, 1961), for an interesting analysis of one way in which this occurs.

Relatively few sources are available on the question of how policy-makers respond to the opinion-submitting process, but the following provide sufficient data on the subject to suggest that further research in this area is feasible and potentially fruitful:

Lewis Anthony Dexter, "What Do Congressmen Hear: The Mail," *Public Opinion Quarterly,* Vol. XX (Spring 1956), pp. 16-27.

Robert Ellsworth Elder, *The Policy Machine: The Department of State and American Foreign Policy* (Syracuse: Syracuse University Press, 1960), esp. Part Three.

Roger Hilsman, "The Foreign-Policy Consensus: An Interim Research Report," *Journal of Conflict Resolution,* Vol. III (December 1959), pp. 361-82.

Martin Kriesberg, "What Congressmen and Administrators Think of the Polls," *Public Opinion Quarterly,* Vol. IX (Fall 1945), pp. 333-37.

Leila Sussmann, "FDR and the White House Mail," *Public Opinion Quarterly,* Vol. XX (Spring 1956), pp. 5-16.

The Mass and Attentive Publics

Numerous works are available on the attitudes and structure of the mass public. The general findings in this area are ably and extensively summarized in Alfred O. Hero, *Americans in World Affairs* (Boston: World Peace Foundation, 1959). Mr. Hero's fifty pages of footnotes also serve as an excellent and exhaustive bibliography on the subject. In addition, one could profitably consult Thomas A. Bailey, *The Man in the Street: The Impact of American Public Opinion on Foreign Policy* (New York: The Macmillan Co., 1948), and William A. Scott and Stephen B. Withey, *The United States and the United Nations: The Public View, 1945-1955* (New York: Manhattan Publishing Co., 1958). An interesting inquiry into mass attitudes toward a new type of foreign policy issue is provided by Gabriel A. Almond, "Public Opinion and Space Technology," *Public Opinion Quarterly,* Vol. XXIV (Winter 1960), pp. 553-72. Equally stimulating is the empirical investigation of the fluctuation in mass moods conducted by Frank L. Klingberg, in "The Historical Alternation of Moods in American Foreign Policy," *World Politics,* Vol. IV (January 1952), pp. 239-73.

As for the attentive public, here the literature is less extensive, although frequently analyses of the mass public contain data and conclusions which pertain to its more attentive segments. Of the few sources which deal directly with the attitudes and behavior patterns of the attentive public, one of the most thorough is Alfred O. Hero, *Voluntary Organizations in World Affairs* (Boston: World Peace Foundation, 1960). Again Mr. Hero's footnotes serve as an excellent source for further bibliographic materials. Also of considerable value is Bernard C. Cohen, *Citizen Education in World Affairs* (Princeton: Center of International Studies, 1953). Some interesting data on a small segment of the attentive public is available in John Fischer, "Self-Portrait of the *Harper* Reader," *Harper's,* Vol. 217 (September 1958).

The Opinion-Making Public

Although numerous studies of particular national leadership groups are available, and while there is a growing volume of inquiries into the interaction of opinion-makers at the community level, there is a relative scarcity of literature on the structure and interaction patterns of the opinion-making public at the national level. One very interesting discussion along these lines is Talcott Parsons, "The

Distribution of Power in American Society," *World Politics,* Vol. X (October 1957), pp. 123-43. This is a critical review of C. Wright Mills, *The Power Elite* (New York: Oxford University Press, 1956), which also concerns itself (in a more eloquent, if not bombastic, fashion) with the question of who exercises control in the American community. Another essay review of Mills's book worthy of consultation is Daniel Bell, "The Power Elite—Reconsidered," *American Journal of Sociology,* Vol. 64 (November 1958), pp. 238-50. Additional general treatments of the subject will be found in the elite series of the Hoover Institute Studies, especially in the introductory volume by Harold D. Lasswell, Daniel Lerner, and C. Easton Rothwell, *The Comparative Study of Elites* (Stanford: Stanford University Press, 1952). A particularly lucid and thorough introduction to the subject is Donald R. Matthews, *The Social Background of Political Decision-Makers* (Garden City: Doubleday and Co., 1954). Highly theoretical discussions of various dimensions of the role played by opinion-makers are available in Raymond A. Bauer, "The Communicator and the Audience," *Journal of Conflict Resolution,* Vol. II (March 1958), pp. 67-77; M. D. Feld, "Political Policy and Persuasion: The Role of Communications from Political Leaders," *Journal of Conflict Resolution,* Vol. II (March 1958), pp. 78-89; Louis Kriesberg, "Societal Coordination by Occupational Leaders," *PROD,* Vol. III (September 1959), pp. 34-36; and James W. Prothro and Charles Grigg, "Societal Coordination by the Educated Minority," *PROD,* Vol. III (January 1960), pp. 7-9. At the more popular and less systematic level it might prove fruitful to peruse Osborn Elliott, *Men at the Top* (New York: Harper & Bros., 1959); John M. Henry (ed.), *The Articulates* (Indianapolis: Bobbs-Merrill Co., 1957); and Floyd Hunter, *Top Leadership U.S.A.* (Chapel Hill: University of North Carolina Press, 1959).

As for general analyses of the national opinion-making

public which concentrate on foreign policy matters, an interesting effort to explore empirically some of Almond's notions is provided by Kenneth P. Adler and Davis Bobrow, "Interest and Influence in Foreign Affairs," *Public Opinion Quarterly*, Vol. XX (Spring 1956), pp. 89-102. Another empirical investigation worthy of careful reading is Harold R. Isaacs, *Scratches On Our Minds: American Images of China and India* (New York: John Day Co., 1958), whereas a broad survey of findings in this area will be found in Alfred O. Hero, *Opinion Leaders in American Communities* (Boston: World Peace Foundation, 1959). An interesting symposium on a foreign opinion-making public is available in Hans Speier and W. Phillips Davison (eds.), *West German Leadership and Foreign Policy* (Evanston: Row, Peterson & Co., 1957). A popular but provocative analysis of a foreign policy organization, the Council of Foreign Relations, composed exclusively of various types of American opinion-makers is Joseph Kraft, "School for Statesmen," *Harper's*, Vol. 217 (July 1958). Another popular and stimulating discussion which takes a critical view of the opinion-making public is David Riesman, "Private People and Public Policy," *Bulletin of the Atomic Scientists*, Vol. 15 (May 1959), pp. 203-8.

Of the many available inquiries into the role of particular segments of the opinion-making public, the following sample is suggestive of the kinds of studies which are primarily oriented toward foreign policy matters:

Raymond A. Bauer and Ithiel de Sola Pool, *American Businessmen and International Trade: Code Book and Data from A Study on Attitudes and Communications* (Glencoe: Free Press, 1960).

Morris Janowitz, "Military Elites and the Study of War," *Journal of Conflict Resolution*, Vol. I (March 1957), pp. 9-18.

Henry A. Kissinger, "The Policymaker and the Intellectual," *The Reporter,* Vol. 20 (March 5, 1959), pp. 30-5.

D. S. McClelland and C. E. Woodhouse, "Businessmen and Foreign Policy," *Southwestern Social Science Quarterly* (March 1959).

William C. Mitchell, "Occupational Role Strains: The American Elective Public Official," *Administrative Science Quarterly,* Vol. III (September 1958), pp. 210-28.

Leila Sussmann, "The Personnel and Ideology of Public Relations," *Public Opinion Quarterly,* Vol. XII (Winter 1948-49), pp. 697-707.

The Communications System

On this subject the literature is almost unmanageable and we can cite only a few of the representative items. Perhaps the most fruitful sources are these three symposia: Bernard Berelson and Morris Janowitz (eds.), *Reader in Public Opinion and Communication* (Glencoe: Free Press, 1953); Daniel Katz, Dorwin Cartwright, Samuel Eldersveld, and Alfred McClung Lee (eds.), *Public Opinion and Propaganda* (New York: Dryden Press, 1954); Wilbur Schramm (ed.), *The Process and Effects of Mass Communication* (Urbana: University of Illinois Press, 1954). As previously noted, an extremely important monograph in this area is Elihu and Paul F. Lazarsfeld, *Personal Influence: The Part Played by People in the Flow of Mass Communications* (Glencoe: Free Press, 1955). An interesting attempt to study the communications system experimentally will be found in Melvin L. De Fleur and Otto N. Larsen, *The Flow of Information: An Experiment in Mass Communication* (New York: Harper & Bros., 1958). As for the operation of the system with respect to foreign policy issues, a general survey is available in Alfred O. Hero, *Mass Media and World Affairs* (Boston: World Peace Foundation, 1959). Again Mr. Hero's elaborate footnotes (pp. 149-87) can be used as an excellent bibliographical source. An extremely provocative discussion of the role played by the press in both the opinion-making and policy-making processes is provided by Douglass Cater, *The Fourth Branch of Government* (Boston: Houghton Mifflin Co., 1959). A very insightful, albeit controversial, discussion of the role played by television can be had in Edward R. Murrow, "A Reporter Talks to His Colleagues," *The Reporter,* Vol. 19 (November 13, 1958). A very useful compilation of quantitative data pertaining to the mass media is provided by Richard E. Chapin, *Mass Communications: A Statistical Analysis* (East Lansing: Michigan State University Press, 1957).